A RECIPE FOR FAITH

Inspire.

DEVOTIONS FOR BUSY YOUNGSTERS

PSALM 34

PAUL MARTIN

Illustrations: Paul Martin.

Other books by this author:
Inspire. A resource for busy youth workers. Volumes 1 & 2.
LEADER'S GUIDE Inspire. Devotions for busy youngsters. Psalm 34
Inspire. Devotions for busy youngsters. Finding Identity. Psalm 139
Inspire. Devotions for busy people. Psalm 34

Cover design adapted from line drawings by Amy Walters
www.amywaltersart.com

Artwork for lightbulb adapted and modified from an original line drawing by Amy Walters. Permission is granted solely for use by Paul Martin in his Inspire series and may not be replicated elsewhere.

Cover Photo: Patrick Buck (Unsplash)

To all you busy youngsters out there.
May you receive all of the good things
that God has in store for you!

Be inspired!

ACKNOWLEDGEMENTS

I would like to thank my wonderful wife Deb, for always being there for me. You are a wonderful wife to me and brilliant mum to our boys. Thank you for coming up with the idea for pics to go with each devotion and allowing me the space to find time to write and draw when I got inspired.

Thank you to Alfie for reading through this book and giving me some handy tips on making sure it relates to people of your age. Henry you are an awesome author! I'm certain that you too will write and publish books of your own! Thank you both for being patient with me when I needed to find time to write.

Thank you to Mum & Dad, for your constant encouragement and support to me in the youth ministry. Thank you for the time you have both spent checking through all the details of this book and offering suggestions about the content and layout.

Thank you Simon Genoe for all of your encouragements in ministry! You keep my mind sharp and challenge me in all the right ways.

Thank you to Carlton Baxter for your many encouragements with my writing endeavours!

Thank you to Richard Lyttle for the great photo that you took of me! Perfect for the back cover pic!

Thank you to Amy Walters for your light bulb line drawing, which has become a logo for my Inspire books. I love the prophetic insight that comes through your art and design work. You are truly gifted.

...and thank you for buying this devotional! I wrote it so that you will find strength and freedom in Jesus to live your life to the full as you depend on God for so much!

ABOUT THIS BOOK

Hello. I'm Paul and I wrote this book for you! I've worked as a Youth Pastor for over 18 years, so I've met a lot of young people over that time (and obviously I was one once). We've often had times to chat as we walk down the road, or boot a football around at the park; discussing all sorts over the years. Pokémon and Star Wars have been talking points as well as God, praying, difficulties with parents, friends or bullies, everything really.

This might be the first time you have ever had a devotional before, so I'll just explain a little of what's going on. A devotional is your chance to take some time out of your day to reflect on God as well as to consider what's going on in your life. I believe God is really interested in your day and wants to be your help, support, guide and friend (as well as your rescuer!). Just by letting Him in to your struggles, stresses and pain (as well as those successful times), you will begin to find He's not only there with you in it all, but actually making a real difference.

So each day there's a verse from Psalm 34 (from the Bible) to read and then there's a bit that I have written where we'll talk about what God might be saying to you. Think of it as a bit of chitchat over an ice cream McFlurry. You'll then have a chance to think about it all and to talk about your thoughts to God. See this as your own personal journey diary with God. So if you want to write in it, underline it or doodle you go for it. I'm often inspired to draw pictures as they can communicate a concept that God wants to teach me. If something comes to mind, even if you can't draw, give it a try!

I've added in some prayer pages for you to write or draw some thoughts to God too. I like to put on a worship song before or after I've read the Bible and then just write or draw.

So I'm praying for you! May you discover how much you are loved and cared for by Father God.

PSALM 34

Of David, when he changed his behaviour before Abimelech, so that he drove him out, and he went away. (See 1 Samuel 21:1-15)

¹ I will bless the Lord at all times;
His praise shall continually be in my mouth.
² My soul makes its boast in the Lord;
let the humble hear and be glad.
³ Oh, magnify the Lord with me,
and let us exalt His name together!

⁴ I sought the Lord, and He answered me;
He delivered me from all my fears.
⁵ Those who look to Him are radiant,
and their faces shall never be ashamed.
⁶ This poor man called, and the Lord heard him;
He saved him out of all his troubles.
⁷ The angel of the Lord encamps around
those who fear Him, and delivers them.

⁸ Oh, taste and see that the Lord is good!
Blessed is the man who takes refuge in Him!
⁹ Oh, fear the Lord, you His saints,
for those who fear Him have no lack!
¹⁰ The young lions suffer want and hunger;
but those who seek the Lord lack no good thing.

¹¹ Come, O children, listen to me;
I will teach you the fear of the Lord.
¹² What man is there who desires life
and loves many days, that he may see good?
¹³ Keep your tongue from evil
and your lips from speaking deceit.
¹⁴ Turn away from evil and do good;
seek peace and pursue it.

¹⁵ The eyes of the Lord are toward the righteous
and His ears toward their cry.
¹⁶ The face of the Lord is against those who do evil,
to cut off the memory of them from the earth.
¹⁷ When the righteous cry for help, the Lord hears
and delivers them out of all their troubles.
¹⁸ The Lord is near to the broken-hearted
and saves the crushed in spirit.

¹⁹ Many are the afflictions of the righteous,
but the Lord delivers him out of them all.
²⁰ He keeps all his bones;
not one of them is broken.
²¹ Affliction will slay the wicked,
and those who hate the righteous will be condemned.
²² The Lord redeems the life of His servants;
none of those who take refuge in Him will be condemned.

THE WHISPER OF FEAR

"David took these words to heart
and was very much afraid,"   (1 Samuel 21:10-15)

They say "desperate times call for desperate measures." Take a moment to imagine that you're a successful warrior. You're a fighter so outstanding that people have sung songs about you and the king together; but now you're out of favour. You've been sneaked out of the city and you're on the run. People are unaware that you are missing, so at least you have a head start.

In a short time you are sure to be pursued. Someone powerful is after you and if they catch up with you, you're doomed. This man was your friend, but now you are twice as much his enemy as you were his friend. Maybe you could escape from this one man; but there is an army ready at the king's command, sure to be despatched at any moment. These men will not give up until they have found you.

It appears there is nowhere to flee; nowhere to hide where they won't find you. So in desperation (maybe even as a stroke of genius), you go for safety in the one place where they are least likely to look for you. Unfortunately there's a small problem with this place you have stopped at; it just so happens to be the capital city of your actual enemies the Philistines. A dangerous place to find safety!

In a previous battle you killed their champion fighter (a history not easy to forget). Plenty of people will want their pound of flesh to avenge his death. So you try to hide your identity disguising yourself as a peasant. Yet those in charge have been alerted to your presence. Their servants are everywhere and in no time you are brought before the king.

You've come a long way from being a shepherd boy out in the country, facing off a giant when everyone else was too fearful to try. But now you have escaped with your life and very little else. Talk about going "from the frying pan into the fire!" So as you are brought to the king of the Philistines you are sure that he will satisfy himself by drawing his sword and killing the slayer of Goliath. This is probably not the time to mention that you know where the sword of Goliath is! Kings were known for their lack of patience as well as their ability to prove their authority with instant executions. The thought of what this king will do terrifies you.

We read the words *"David took these words to heart and was very much afraid..."* The servants of the king are quick to remind him of David's warrior status. "Pssst! Hasn't he killed loads of Philistine soldiers? Fathers, husbands and sons of ours who will never return to their families?" Instantly David feels vulnerable, unarmed and at the mercy of the king of his enemies. Fear takes the opportunity and whispers in his ear "You know what?? You're done for!" And in this moment of pressure David listens to the whispers, he believes the voice of fear. Panic seizes David and he loses sight of the truth that God has promised him a future!

It's after this moment of terror that David writes one of the most powerful Psalms in the Bible. It's powerful because it contains a way out from the negative place that fear can take in our lives. David found a place of freedom from anxiety through God's power and wrote about it. I believe that God wants to lead you into a place where you find yourself depending more and more on your Heavenly Father for all that you need, so that fear will find it hard to take hold of your heart.

As we begin this journey away from fear and towards faith, why not commit to pray this with me:

Father God. I need you. I understand the negative effect that some fears can have over my life. During the next few months please lead me to find the way out from the harmful fears that hold me down. I need You to lead me into a place where I will discover safety and freedom.

FEAR IN THE HEART

"David took these words to heart..."   (1 Samuel 21:10-15)

I wonder if ours is the generation that has written more words than any other in history? Think about it for a moment, we're always on our smartphones or tablets communicating to our friends, writing posts, comments or blogs. But with all this writing, comes the risk of being misunderstood. I'm sure you've had a text from someone and thought the person was being rude, just because it was written in a certain way. So helpfully, someone invented emojiis! A little smiley face, a sad face, winking face or even a love heart can fill in the emotional blanks that can be missed by the words we use to communicate.

We all know that a heart emoji communicates love or caring feelings and when the Bible talks about "the heart" it's describing more than just a feeling; it represents that deep part of us. It's where we decide things, it what moves us to cry or laugh, our motivations come from the heart and with it we can feel vulnerable or afraid. So what did it mean, *"David took these words to heart?"*

Remember we read yesterday about David's desperate attempt to escape from King Saul's imminent man hunt and how David ended up in Philistine territory? He's taken to Achish, king of the Philistines, whose servants bring up David's warrior exploits against these Philistines. They argue the point: "Can we trust David our enemy to live among us?"

David understands that if the answer to this question is "No," then there is no alternative but to kill him. The seriousness of his situation gives rise to fear in his heart. Who wouldn't be afraid at this most desperate situation? And with panic starting to surge within, David can see only the negative outcomes that fear has persuaded him are just a matter of time.

You know fear can actually be a positive thing. Fear can alert us to danger. It can stop us from walking too near a cliff edge, looking into the mouth of a crocodile, or swimming with hungry sharks. That is what fear is meant for, to help us to avoid danger.

But there are times when fear can be triggered in us when we perceive we're in danger even where there isn't any; our mind becomes anxious and the body physically reacts. Maybe we have an increased heart rate, we find breathing or swallowing more difficult and we might feel sweaty or cold. It's possible that taking on negative thoughts into our hearts can reduce our capacity to do things like being brave. Even just coping with normal situations can become more difficult. When fear starts to take control it can also affect our motivation as well as our abilities.

A person who takes to heart anxious thoughts will act differently. Have you ever worried about something and thought, "What if this happens??" Our mind starts to process worst-case scenarios and as a result our capacity to have a joyful life is reduced. Worry leads to anxiety and fear.

Now it's easy to say this, but actually David wasn't in as much danger as he feared. A while back (with God's help) he had defeated Goliath the giant using a sling and a stone! And there is another reason why David need not panic; the prophet Samuel had told David he would be king and God's promise to him had not yet been fulfilled! God gave David a way out, it wasn't pretty; but he lived to fight another day!

So I want to ask you this: who are you more ready to listen to when bad news hits? Do you fear the worst? Does panic try to seize you? Why not remind yourself that you are being looked after by a rescuer called Jesus, who wants you to trust Him to provide for your needs and a way through troubles? Don't give up and think that terrible things will happen. God has a way through for you. As you reflect on this, turn the page as there's a prayer space for you to hand over to God those things that worry you.

THANKS

THINGS GOD HAS DONE

GOD YOU ARE

IN MY LIFE YOU HAVE

I trust that you are:

WHAT I LOVE ABOUT YOU IS...

HELP ME WITH

I devote
this
to you

SPEAK LOUDER THAN YOUR FEARS

"I will bless the Lord at all times;
His praise shall continually be in my mouth."   (Psalm 34:1)

I bought this really amazing speaker. You know the type. They connect to your smartphone or computer and are small enough to carry around, but loud enough to blast out any tune enabling you to hear every bit with absolute clarity. It's great for wall to wall sound in your bedroom. Trouble is though, when I try to recreate that sound in a medium sized or large meeting room, even with the volume up to full it sounds so much quieter. If you're on the other side of a room full of people you can't even make out the words. The boom of the volume is no longer attracting the attention of the people in the room next to me.

Worry can be a bit like the sound from that speaker. Imagine that your worries and fears are blasting out loads of negative noise into your mind. It can feel like that is all you can hear and it's tough to block out its effects. It begins to process around in your mind like a song on repeat.

But what if you were to take those same worries or fears into a bigger room? What if you took a step outside of your thinking and began to invite God into the situation and think about God, His greatness and His love for you? Suddenly the sounds of your fears are in a bigger space. You will notice that they are beginning to turn into wee background music that you can choose to ignore. Suddenly you feel strengthened, empowered, encouraged and faith starts to rise in your heart.

How is that possible? It's all about the heart. When we fill up our heart full of God, fear gets pushed out to the edges where it ceases to have that power and influence over us. You see the sort of fears that we are talking about can sometimes be thoughts put there by an enemy who wants to make us weak. At these times we need a spiritual strength to fight back that only God can give.

So our Psalm begins with the words *"I will bless the Lord at all times. His praise shall continually be in my mouth."* You know these two sentences actually say the same thing using different words. It's like God is turning up the volume on His speaker and saying "You need to hear this!! So I'm going to say it twice! Praise out loud is really important!!" Maybe you know that you can pray to God with your thoughts; He hears those as well as the ones we say out loud. But there is this added dynamic when we use our voice to talk to God. We hear what we are saying, God hears what we are saying (obviously) and our enemy hears what we are saying. When we have words of faith and speak them out loud something happens. The volume of our fears decreases as our minds enter into God's room, God's space.

Obviously you know it's not about the noise you use, but rather that you vocalise the truth about who God is. Not only does it put our situation into perspective, it also reminds us who God is. When we speak out truth, inside our heart the cogs of faith start to turn! Something happens and God the Holy Spirit speaks His inspired words into our heart, causing us to feel braver about the situation we are concerned about. We'll realise that God is working in our lives and guiding us through our difficulties and leading us to the solutions for our problems.

So speak louder than your fears! Say it out loud! Remind yourself who God is! Okay. You might be thinking, "Talk to myself?? That's crazy!" Well, it's not just yourself that you are talking to! The Bible talks about encouraging ourselves with God's words; and even in Lamentations 3:24 it says "I say to myself, "The Lord is my portion; therefore I will wait for Him" (NIV).

On the next page there's some space to do just this. Why not think through some of the words in the Bible about God and whatever inspires you, note it down and read it out loud! Declare the praises of God!

"for **He** is the

living God,

ENDURING FOREVER;

His kingdom shall never be destroyed,

and His **dominion**

shall be to the end.

He **delivers** and rescues;

He works **signs** and **wonders**

in **heaven** and on **earth**,"

Why not find a Psalm that declares the truth about God and write it out with your own style of writing? As you write, think about the words and what they tell you about God.

#Day4

DECLARING HIS PRAISES

"I will bless the Lord at all times;
His praise shall continually be in my mouth."   (Psalm 34:1)

Let's talk about habits; those things we do regularly, because we did them yesterday, the day before and the day before. You know… things like getting up on time for school. And you know; if you go to bed and get up at regular times, after a while you'll just wake up at the right time, because your body clock has got used to it. Developing habits like waking up at the same time each day without an alarm only happens because you've done it on purpose. Maybe you've had to remind yourself to do it to start with and after a few weeks you got used to it, so you don't need reminding now, because you've gotten into the habit of doing it. Stuff like eating an apple instead of a Mars bar, holding off spending your pocket money all at once or remembering to check your bag the night before you have sports at school. They are all habits we grow into.

I get up on a Saturday morning to go on a 5K run every week. This is the first time I've missed it in about 15 weeks and it feels so weird not doing it. It's a good habit that I've only got used to because I've done it continually week in week out. I know that when I go running next week my body won't freak out halfway round the course, because I'm used to it.

Can we look at the same verse we read yesterday? Is that okay? Yesterday we talked about speaking out the truth about God. Our fears shrink back as the truth about God is spoken and the lies of the enemy fade. The reason why our fears sometimes gain so much space in our minds is that some fears do actually alert us to real danger. Yet the problem is that a lot of our worries and fears that appear to be alerting us to danger are actually telling us lies. There is no danger. But when we feel we face uncertain or unknown situations, fear shouts at us with possible negative outcomes. We can end up believing these lies and get unnecessarily anxious. Therefore we need to identify the truth.

If you've ever had an argument with someone and discover they are telling lies, as soon as the truth is presented what happens to the lie? It disappears. People stop believing it. It has no power anymore.

This is why it is important to remind ourselves of the truth about God. When we discover who He is, we will come to realise His influence in our lives and how He will not let the lies of fear materialise. He will provide for you as you trust Him. But it is easy to forget what God is like. Especially as we hear so many things said about God that are not true!

So David, this man who temporarily forgot God and became so afraid in the presence of the king of the Philistines; what does he say is a good habit to have? *"at all times… continually"* to have God's praise in our mouths. By declaring God's praise on a regular basis, our minds are hearing it, the enemy is hearing it, God is hearing it and we are remembering it. And as we do this repeatedly our confidence will grow in God's ability to deal with the things that worry us. The enemy shrinks back, as his lie has no power when the truth about God is presented.

Listening to fear is a bad habit which needs to be broken. It is broken by taking on some good habits. Regular, ongoing praise will lead you to know God more and to discover so much of His goodness.

Shall we talk to God about all this?

Father God. I want to see You for who You are. Would You help me to develop the practice of declaring Your praises every day? Thank You that You are present with me now. Please reveal more of what You are like. Show me more of You I pray.

BOASTING IN THE BEST

"My soul makes its boast in the Lord;

let the humble hear and be glad."   (Psalm 34:2)

A number of years back my older brother bought season tickets to see Arsenal play football at Highbury in London. We'd go and find some nearby street to park the car (actually miles from the venue) and walk in. As we got closer to the stadium, more and more people wearing the familiar colours of red and white would appear. First it was a couple and then a group, then several groups, until we found ourselves in a crowd.

It was quite daunting being in a crowd full of supporters, but even more overwhelming than that was the singing. I could never really understand it myself. You'd be walking down the street and some lad would be singing "And it's Arsenal (Arsenoool), Arsenal FC! We're by far the greatest team, the world has ever seen." And I'm there thinking, no football team could ever be that great to motivate me to sing that about them in public. It's cool if people want to do that, but my heart just doesn't get *that* excited about a team for me to praise them like that.

And it got me thinking… why do people sing at football matches? So the Arsenal song is about encouraging their team, by saying "We believe in you. You are the best team there is." It's also meant to discourage the opposition, "You'll never be able to beat the greatest team in the world." So a lot about what football fans sing, is to do with boasting about how good their team or players are. A boast is to give glory.

Often we think about boasting as someone talking very highly about themselves, often about their own achievements, which let's face it, no one likes a boaster! But boasting about God is something very different.

First of all it comes from within, *"My soul makes its boast."* That inner part of you, your heart where you decide things, chooses to consider God and express it. This is an important moment where you can turn into words your expressions of appreciation and devotion to God. Declaring the truth about God and declaring that you believe it is your heart response to God. It's all very well saying you know Jesus Christ was a man in history; that is truth. However to say you believe He is the Son of God and that there is none greater than Him, that is expressing the truth in faith. You are saying that your soul has made a connection with God and your words boast about who He is and the great things He has done.

Ok. You might be thinking, "How do I get my heart to boast about God? I would never know what to say!" Great question. A lot of people never get close to God when they pray because of this very thing. So how's it done?

It starts by thinking on just one thing, or rather person, God. Let all else take second place for a while. The best way to discover what He is like is to read somewhere in the Bible that describes Him well. Take a look at Psalm 103. Why not read a sentence that describes God and think about it? Ask the Holy Spirit to show you what Jesus and Father God are like. Then just wait and see what thoughts come to mind as you read that little sentence. Then when something comes to mind, tell God about it and how it describes Him. Turn these words into adoration as your soul shows its appreciation for God. As we do this God comes close.

Do you remember the other thing that boasting in your team does? It discourages the opposition! Our enemy who wants to sow lies and fears into our hearts can't get close because of our one-to-ones with God. Our hearts are too full of God for the enemy to get a look in! We become a much tougher nut to crack when we boast in the Lord. Say it with your mouth, not just your thoughts – even if it's just a whisper! You will hear what you are saying and realise that God is at work in your heart!

Why not find Psalm 103 in the Bible? Choose just one sentence then look at the next page of this book for an inspired prayer time...

PRAYER SPACE

Why not take this moment to write God a letter? Forget asking Him for anything at the moment (although He absolutely loves to give good gifts to His children!) But just for a moment begin writing a letter to Father God, noticing what He is like and what you love about who He is.

Dear Father God,

PRAYER SPACE

If you feel inspired to draw something, maybe a picture about what God is like may come to mind. The Bible uses loads of picture language to describe God... a refuge and place of safety, a rock that is a firm foundation, a shield as our protector. God is all those things and many more besides!

Once you have something written down, why not read it out so your ears can hear it? It'll do you the world of good! Let the humble hear and be glad!

MUSIC TO YOUR EARS

"...let the humble hear and rejoice."   (Psalm 34:2)

Do you ever get those moments when you just feel like singing? You've got your headphones on with your favourite tune. It doesn't matter who's around or if it sounds any good, you just want to sing along. What about the echo you get when singing in the shower? The acoustics make the worst singer feel like they're worth a go on the X Factor! On a good day I've sung along to the words of "Living on a prayer" by Bon Jovi (not sure it was a good day for those outside the bathroom). Obviously headphones and the shower don't mix! But yeah, the melody is just in your head and you just have to sing along.

There's a melody that God wants you to catch a hold of. It's a song of heaven which declares that His Kingdom is breaking into our world. You know, the Psalms are actually songs. In Old Testament days they didn't have the Bible on smartphones or even in nicely printed books. To discover God's word they would go to the Temple where it would be read. So the Psalms were songs written to music; and people would learn to sing them. I'm sure when you were young you learned your ABC? I expect you were taught it in a song, so that you would be able to remember it easily. I can still remember the tune!

Psalm 34 is a song declaring the truth about God so that we may be encouraged that we are cared for, watched over and loved by Almighty God. Our fears don't have a chance! In it contains the evidence that God looks out for us. We're also encouraged that when we search more for who He is for us, this leads us to be delivered from our fears!

In the bit we read today we see it is talking about the "humble." This describes those who have been brought down by their circumstances. Other versions say *"Let the afflicted hear and rejoice,"* which describes someone who is experiencing ongoing suffering. I know if I was afflicted I would find it difficult to rejoice, but that is the very thing encouraged to do. Why? There are two reasons:

Firstly you have reason to be encouraged because your answer is coming; and secondly because as you declare and thank in faith you are expressing a trust in God that He is willing to meet your needs.

Imagine you have a younger brother or sister. They are doing their homework and are struggling with a Maths problem and you know that you are able to help them with it. So you go up to them and ask what the problem is. Imagine they don't want to tell you. It's hard to be able to help them if they won't let you in. What if you take a look anyway and begin to explain to them how to do the sum, but they don't believe you have the right answer even when you tell them? Putting our trust in God is a little like your younger brother or sister putting their trust in you to solve the Maths problem. We have to let God in and believe that He knows what He is doing, instead of being afraid that His solution will be the wrong one.

So why not take in deeply this melody of heaven that comes through the words of the Psalm. It's more than a song; it describes the ethos of heaven – the way God's Kingdom works. It's a Kingdom where God is the King and where those who look to the King for safety are welcomed and provided for as Princes and Princesses. Oh how much we can boast in God and His goodnesses!

May the words of this Psalm encourage you to see how much your Heavenly Father loves you and will work on your behalf as you let Him in.

Father God. I need you. Please help me to understand the ethos of Heaven, this melody that communicates how You do things. Help me to leave fear behind and to take steps closer to You. In Jesus' name!

UNDER THE MICROSCOPE

"Oh, magnify the Lord with me,
and let us exalt His name together!"   (Psalm 34:3)

Something freaked me out the other day. I was in a science place and they had this digital microscope for us to try out. They had some rocks which we could place under the microscope lens and it would show up on a screen. It was super cool, although after a while the rocks got a bit boring, so me and Henry (he's nine years old), started thinking of what else we could put under there. Things like dead bugs and bogies came to mind, but since neither of those was available, we just focused the scope on our fingers.

It was incredible! The screen showed up our finger prints like massive ridges, and tiny little specks could be seen so clearly. Unfortunately it was then that I got bit of a shock. I caught a look under my finger nail and there was some seriously weird black crusty stuff that was even worse than a bogey! It was disgusting! I couldn't believe it as I'd been biting my nails just the other day! I needed soap and I needed it right away!

Okay before I make you feel ill, I'm going somewhere with this thought... You see it's possible to focus in on the wrong things and to magnify them out of all proportion. I'd gone days, weeks, years, maybe even my whole life with crusty bits under my nails. The fact is we carry around all sorts of crud under our nails – which is why hand-washing before food is a good idea! But, you know we don't worry about those things unless we notice them; and when we didn't notice them, they weren't an issue.

When we begin to worry about stuff, we can accidentally magnify them to the point where we get spooked or freak out. Fear is faith in the wrong things. It is a belief that our troubles are bigger than God. Often we have only come to this conclusion because we have put our fears under the microscope and thought about them way too much, which has had the effect of magnifying them.

David had his enemies. I guess if we were to take that one story of David being before the king of Gath on its own and put that under the micro scope, it would appear that he had more enemies than friends. But that wasn't true. The people sang songs about him, they loved him. He was chosen to be king. God had a plan for him. Yes there were a few powerful people against him; but as we see, they couldn't harm him because God was his protector. If you read on from 1 Samuel 21, you will see the challenges he faces and how God meets them all for him.

It's a funny word "magnify," especially when it's talking about God. What does it really mean? Well, they didn't have microscopes in those days; but to magnify was to discover the evidence about a person that makes them great and to declare it. By discovering the goodness of God, His great works and declaring them is bringing God glory, it is magnifying God; showing people His greatness.

Now here's the important bit... when we declare these things we are saying we agree with the evidence provided. Sometimes fear can provide false evidence by saying "You've failed in the past, you're no good and it's going to happen to you again." That's a lie. Don't believe it! Replace that lie with the truth.

This is your moment to bring counter evidence to declare that God is greater, that He is working on your behalf. You'll find the evidence in the Bible, in your life, by looking at creation; there's plenty of evidence to put under the microscope.

Shall we pray? *Father God. I thank You that the Bible declares that You are the King over all. Nothing can separate me from Your love for me. You have good plans to prosper me and not to harm me. You make all things work together for my good according to Your purposes. I know that You are always working and that You will provide for all my needs!*

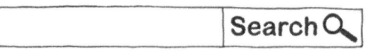

#Day8

SEARCHING FOR I AM

"I sought the Lord and He answered me…" (Psalm 34:4)

I'm sure you're well used to searching for stuff. Nowadays it's so easy. Want to get your dad a vintage toy for Christmas or a special box of chocs for mum? A quick search online will get you a price. Or maybe you're talking with a friend about a particular actor whose name you can't remember. It takes just a few seconds to find the answer. It's quick; it's easy, no time wasted.

Well, it didn't used to be that way! Before the internet there was a phone book called the "Yellow Pages." You'd have to look under the list for retailers, and then look for the type of shop. Once you'd found it in the list you would either call them up or pop into the shop in the hope they would have what you wanted. If it was information you were looking for, you'd have to go to the library! It took some searching.

Yesterday we talked about discovering the evidence of God's greatness in order to "magnify" God and truly understand who He is. David tells us in the Psalm *"I sought the Lord"* and we could ask the question "Did he lose God?" or "Was God hiding from him?" Neither of those is what David is getting at.

What David was after, was for God to be close to him. You know when you are getting to know a friend. You take time to be around them. When you meet up, you might talk about what someone said to you that day, a clip you saw on TV, or something that happened to you. It's relationship; and that's what Jesus invites us to with Him. It might be that when you're talking to your friend, they tell you that maybe their Gran is sick or they are going through a hard time. You might say to them "I'm here for you," and "let me know if you need anything or want to chat."

Those words encourage your friend that they know who you are for them at this time.

So when we seek the Lord, we are after God showing us who He is for us in whatever we are facing. This is a great question to ask God "Who are You for me in this?"

You see, God wants you to seek Him so He can reveal what He is like to you. Then you'll know in your heart that He is with you and how He is working on your behalf.

There's a key phrase in the Bible where God reveals what He is like. This phrase always begins with "I am." Jesus used it when He said *"I am the way, the truth and the life,"* describing that He leads us to God the Father, He is the true Son of God and that He is the source of life. So maybe you decide to take some time to seek God and you are uncertain about the future, you might ask Him "Who are You for me in this?" Maybe God will bring to your mind "I am the way," and you are assured that Jesus is guiding you through those uncertain times and your heart is filled with peace about it all, knowing your future is secure.

There's loads of these "I am" sayings in the Old Testament. "I am the Lord who heals you" tells us of God's power to make us physically well. "I am the God who sees," (Genesis 16:13) communicating that God sees your situation and will bring you justice. Now just like when we talked about searching for things, God loves to speak immediately and yet at other times He leads us on a journey of discovery which takes a bit longer. How do we search for God then?

So let God reveal to you who He is by reading about Him and think deeply as you read, so that when you come up against a difficulty you can remind yourself "I don't need to be stressed about this, God says 'I am your provider.' You'll find Abraham calling a place "The Lord will provide" in Genesis 22:14, and with him you can say "I know that in the place of testing my Father God will provide for me." Now as you turn the page I want to lead you into an exercise in hearing from God...

PRAYER SPACE

You can do this literally anywhere! You don't have to get into a "spiritual zone" or anything like that. God loves to talk to us in a way that is in the natural every day. So even if you're in a coffee house, it's cool, God can speak to you here too.

So all I want you to do is to read the bit of Psalm 34 that we've got to so far…

¹ I will bless the Lord at all times;
His praise shall continually be in my mouth.
² My soul makes its boast in the Lord;
let the humble hear and be glad.
³ Oh, magnify the Lord with me,
and let us exalt His name together!

⁴ I sought the Lord, and He answered me;

And in your heart (so it doesn't have to be out loud), ask the Lord to speak to you and to show you who He is.

You might be thinking, "How do I know if God is speaking to me?" There's two important things to realise about God speaking. Firstly a lot of people expect a vision or a dream, but God also speaks to us in our thoughts. For example, if I were to get you to think of a piece of cake, you would see it in your minds-eye, but it wouldn't be in physical form in front of your eyes. God often speaks in our mind's eye, with pictures or words.

Secondly, I often recognise God speaking randomly and not along my current train of thought. So I might be thinking about what I am about to do next, and then a God idea just pops into my head. It's random, I wasn't trying to think of something, I could be reading or just waiting for something and then in comes that thought; be it a word, an idea, a phrase or a picture and I just give it my attention, write it down and God will develop it as I write. Of course once I've written it, if it doesn't make sense or contradicts the Bible, then it's not God and it goes in the bin! But that actually doesn't happen that much, as God loves to talk to His children!

Anyway… back where we were. Have another read of those verses across the page… Now in your heart (so it doesn't have to be out loud), ask the Lord to speak to you and to show you who He is. Write or draw what comes to mind. If it's just one word, that's a start!

#Day9

DON'T BE AFRAID

"I sought the Lord and He answered me
and delivered me from all my fears." (Psalm 34:4)

Some time ago I had an attack of fear. Following a staff meeting I discovered that my job was under review. Someone high up in the organisation believed that my job should completely change and I left that meeting concerned that I would be out of a job. I felt it was completely the wrong decision, but I felt powerless to be able to do anything about it. But more than that, it weighed heavy on me. I felt a tightening in my chest, like a stress or fear. Then whenever I thought about the situation a wave of panic would hit me. Not a nice feeling at all. My fears were getting to me.

But I remember the moment. I was praying on my bed and as I got up to get on with my day, I felt God speak to me very strongly "Don't be afraid." It gives me goose bumps just talking about it. It was just a thought in my mind, but as those three words came into my mind I felt a peace inside and a strength to face things at work. It was powerful.

Well, things developed over a significant period of time (probably more than a year). Occasionally I would hear things that had been said about it and get updates on the progress. Sometimes there were worrying developments; but whenever that happened I would say to my fears, "The Lord says to me 'Don't be afraid,' so I refuse to be afraid." Again my heart would fill with peace.

You see the Bible reveals God to us as a rescuer, a deliverer from evil and a Saviour. He absolutely loves His children and will give us what we need to make it through those tough times. No doubt we all have to face tough times; it is part of life. However the Bible tells us about God in Psalm 23:5 *"You prepare a table before me in the presence of my enemies;"* which means that in the presence of fear, God is ready to provide all we need. Imagine the enemy trying to rob us of our peace, and there we are happily sitting down eating away enjoying God's peace about it all.

"I sought the Lord and He answered me and delivered me from all my fears." Why have we been looking at praise and discovering who God is as the antidote for fear? It is because He is the only one who is able to shield us from its attacks and provide for us to do well, when in all honesty we should be a complete mess! Here is a promise for you from the Lord. "I will deliver you from all of your fears. Say to your fears 'The Lord says "Do not be afraid." Therefore be gone fear in Jesus' name!'"

This is not about saying magic words. As we seek God and discover who He is, our connection with Him brings freedom and the power to say those things with authority. Does that mean you have to be super-spiritual and pray five hours-a-day? No it means that in your everyday living you invite God into your space. Ask Him to be your deliverer. Take time with Him and you will gain from him the strength you need for today. Don't worry about tomorrow. One day at a time. Trust Him for the next day.

Maybe you are wondering how my job situation turned out? The plans came to nothing! And the person high up in the organisation stepped down from their job!

Fear can be a force for evil. But we can come against it in the name of the Lord. There will be trials and like that picture on the other side of the page, times when things seem to be closing in on us. However, we are protected by the King upon the throne, who is also the best loving Father we could ever have. Shall we talk to Him now?

Father God. I thank You that it says in the Bible a lot of times "Don't be afraid," because You want us to be free from negative fears that lie to us about dangers that aren't real. Thank You that Your word tells me that You can deliver me from all my fears. I give them to You now.

WITH RADIANT FACES

"Those who look to Him are radiant," (Psalm 34:5)

There's a high chance that like me, you too will one day get to marry your beloved. I remember it like it was yesterday; that moment as I stood at the front of the church, looking down the aisle with my brother Dave as my best man standing beside me. I waited with anticipation to see my wife-to-be as news came of her arrival. Then I caught a glimpse of her; seeing her took my breath away. She was stunning. There she was gliding up the aisle with the most enchanting smile, eyes fixed on me.

At that moment everything became a blur... no I'm not using sentimental language, it all became a blur, because a wee tear filled up my eye and my contact lens fell out onto the floor! Thankfully, when planning the wedding I thought it was worth handing Dave a spare lens in case things got emotional. During the first song Dave got out a new lens and I saw her close up... laughing at me.

We just read the words "Those who look to Him are radiant," words that aptly described Debs my bride on that special day. People notice the groom and the best man and the ushers at a wedding, but it is the bride that most people remember. She is a picture of beauty. That is a day that we aim to look our best. Those who are radiant have faces shining with joy and people notice, as it is such a pleasant thing to behold.

But hang on a sec... weren't we just talking about people going through times of fear? Normally when tough times hit, we don't tend to look our best. Worry has a look about it and it certainly isn't radiance!

34

God is offering us a choice. We can either look to our fears; and go through various scenarios in our minds, "What if he says this?" or "What if they ask me to do this?" or "What if this happens?" Or we can fix our eyes on Jesus and look to Him. Just as my bride was looking to me and her face radiated joy, so as we put our trust in Jesus during the tough times, letting go of tendencies to worry; a joy will come to our hearts and it will show on our faces.

This is a promise from Father God to you. When you "look to Him;" He will be the One guiding your life as your source of strength, so you can face your fears with confidence. You'll soon see that your fears are lying about the outcome of your situation. Jesus is working on your behalf and He is in charge of the outcome, to deliver you from evil.

Take a look at Luke 12:22-31 to see what Jesus Himself says. You know it's easy to be concerned about tomorrow and be filled with dread. But actually there isn't a thing we can do about tomorrow's tasks until tomorrow comes around. So if you are preparing for tomorrow, if it's revising for exams, preparing to do a show, planning for an interview, or whatever, your job today is to prepare and not to worry. Your job tomorrow is to do. So why not approach today's tasks today with joy, knowing that Father God is getting things ready for tomorrow.

There is one other thing we can do about tomorrow and that is pray. Tell Jesus about your worries, fears and concerns, as well as your hopes. The Bible says *"Cast your cares upon the Lord, for He cares for you"* (1 Peter 5:7). Maybe you have a busy time ahead of you and you don't know how you will fit it all in.

In my role as Youth Pastor I've planned a fair few events in my time. And you know what? There's a whole lot of variables in planning those bad boys. I won't even start with the list – too much to go wrong! In the end I felt God speak to me and say "Just let Me fill in the gaps that you can't." I began to ask Him to do that. And you know what? So many times the things I didn't have covered got covered, as God stepped in where I wasn't enough. He wants you to lean on Him in this way too. So why not ask?

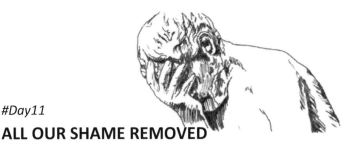

#Day11

ALL OUR SHAME REMOVED

"Those who look to Him are radiant,
and their faces shall never be ashamed."   (Psalm 34:5)

I'm going to tell you about something really embarrassing that happened to me when I was a teenager. I remember when I was about 12 years old. It was Christmas and we were on a school trip to see Peter Pan at the Half Moon Theatre in East London. We'd stepped off the bus and all lined up outside, before getting the go ahead to go into the venue. Quite an exciting time, everyone was a buzz with Christmas just around the corner.

Well we all got inside and found our seats; but it wasn't long before someone noticed a strange smell. My friend sitting next to me asked me if I could smell poo. I couldn't smell a thing as I had a blocked nose, so I just thought he was on a wind up and didn't really give it much thought. Soon those in front of me were saying they could smell something nasty too. So at this moment I decided they couldn't all be wrong and it was worth checking around. I looked down to check my shoes, just to put my mind at rest and was horrified to see I had a big lump of poo sticking out from the bottom of my shoe! Talk about embarrassment and shame!

Anything similar happened to you? I'm sure it has!! That feeling of shame when you mess up can be difficult to shake off; especially when other people know when you did wrong. It's easy to feel like all eyes are on you, thinking about what you did, disapproving of you in their thoughts. Yes I've been there too. God knows all about shame.

The Bible tells us that the very reason Jesus came to earth, was to take away our shame. A good man once said, "Jesus didn't come to rub in our sins, He came to rub them out!" God in His kindness sees that we mess up. God understands that we are human and says, "I have a gift for you. I want to take away your shame." I imagine David felt shame (1 Samuel 21:10-15) having to act in a humiliating manner in order to avoid execution from the king of Gath. Though afterward when David was long gone and the king finally discovered that David was acting... I would have loved to have been a fly on the wall to have seen that! When our shame is taken away it is an incredible moment.

We read *"Those who look to Him are radiant, and their faces shall never be ashamed."* Sometimes the fear of embarrassment and shame can hold us back from attempting something that challenges us. We noticed yesterday that as we look to Jesus and follow His guidance in our lives, a joy comes to our hearts that can be seen on our faces. Yet when we are influenced and guided by our fears; we become anxious, stressed and full of worry. Yes our fears can actually guide us. We can let the fear of failure or embarrassment persuade us to turn down an opportunity to sing solo in the choir, to stand up confidently in the face of a bully, to do a speech in an assembly or whatever your challenge is. But the thing is you are gifted. God gave you the ability to create some incredible things, so don't let fear hold you back.

Maybe you've been reading this book and you haven't been able to really identify any fears yet; that is until now! We've talked a bit about overcoming fear quite a bit so far; so it might be worth you taking a look at some of the earlier bits in this book to identify the steps in order to overcome fear through praise.

Here in Psalm 34:5 is a promise to you from God. God promises that when you "go for it" in whatever challenge you face, as you look to Him for help and guidance; He will make sure that the risks you take will be rewarded with honour because you are honouring Him.

We need to pray this through... *Father God. I thank you that I am a very talented individual. I know this because You have given me gifts and abilities and You only give good gifts. Help me to find my confidence in You so that those liars of fear and embarrassment don't hold me back! I love You!*

#Day12

A BIRD'S EYE VIEW

*"This poor man cried, and the Lord heard him
     and saved him out of all his troubles."* (Psalm 34:6)

Sometimes I wish I was 17 again. Well actually, maybe a bit younger. "What do you mean? Are you crazy?? You want to do school again?" I hear you ask. You might say, "I wish someone would save me out of my school troubles! And you want to go back??"

Let me explain... Of course I pretty much hated high school when I was a boy, but if I knew then what I know now, I think I would have done a lot better. I think they call this "hindsight," which is looking back after the event with the wisdom of how to do things differently.

I imagine my French would be how do they say?... "très bon!" (very good) having visited France a number of times and attempted to buy a cake and go on the underground train. If I was doing Design and Technology, I would now be a wood work or metal work specialist and since I have done a lot of DIY I am no longer afraid of the drill! Science would also see me being a lot less fearful when it was time for everyone to turn on the Bunsen Burners! Now I'm old I would appreciate History a lot more and Physical Education would be something of a bonus as I never get to play footy or rugger with people anymore! I might even learn to swim if I got another chance at swimming lessons (yes I was afraid of the deep water). And the school bully, well I would certainly have some things to say to him, as well as a few moves to take down the lads I would meet from the opposing school on the way home.

You know, sometimes we need someone with experience to remind us that God is faithful! We have the words of David in a very troublesome situation, where he's escaped two kings and he describes himself as *"this poor man,"* reflecting how weak he felt in the presence of such powerful men. Like David, we might feel weak and helpless at school and find the stress of our workload hard to bear, or the balancing of home life and school life might be tough to cope with. It's in our weakness that God supports us in our troubles. We'd love it if we had super abilities to help us breeze through school with all its issues, but it's in our weakness that God wants us to lean on Him. O wow and He can do some incredible miracles! God is able to take you through all that stuff, to the other side of your troubles. Then you too can look back and say, "Surely God was with me in it all, because I couldn't have done it in my own strength."

So when you're feeling weak, God's promise to you is that He hears you the moment you talk to Him. Do you feel like your words to God are just bouncing off the ceiling back at you? He is with you, present in the room whether you feel He is there or not. His promise is that He will save you out of your troubles. David with his hindsight looks back as says "This poor man cried, and the Lord heard him and saved him out of His troubles."

If we were to take a bird's eye view of our situation and to see things as God sees them (both the start and the finish), we would feel a lot different about our difficulties. I heard this song recently which helps us to picture God's perspective on the things we are going through. It goes "This is how I fight my battles. It may look like I'm surrounded, but I'm surrounded by You."[a]

When we feel we're toast; that our circumstances have become too much to bear, God wants you to know He's not far away. He's right close, with you in the struggle. He's always working on our behalf. So be confident in Him. Though tough times may be ahead, He will save you out of your troubles – all of your troubles.

I have something I'd like you to give a try. There's another prayer space over the page with something called a word cloud. Why not turn up Psalm 46 and have a think about what God is like. Then just write the words or phrases down as they come to mind, big or small horizontal or vertical...

a. Fight my battles. Michael W. Smith ©2017 Rocketown Records/The Fuel Music

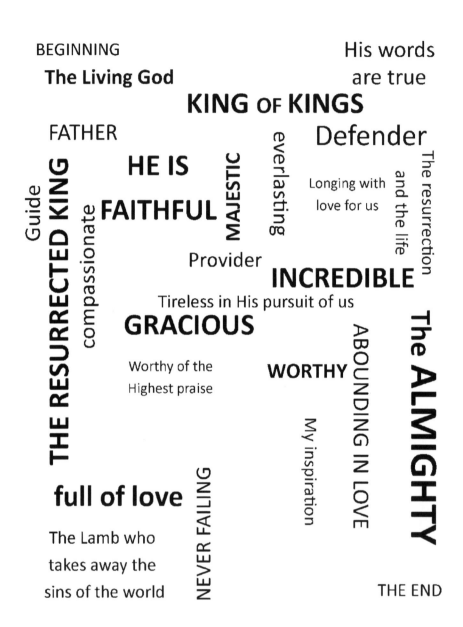

BEGINNING His words

The Living God are true

KING OF KINGS

FATHER Defender

everlasting

HE IS MAJESTIC

The resurrection and the life

Guide **THE RESURRECTED KING** compassionate **FAITHFUL**

Longing with love for us

Provider

INCREDIBLE

Tireless in His pursuit of us

GRACIOUS

Worthy of the Highest praise

WORTHY ABOUNDING IN LOVE

The **ALMIGHTY**

My inspiration

full of love NEVER FAILING

The Lamb who takes away the sins of the world

THE END

PRAYER SPACE – WORD CLOUD

SURROUNDED BY ANGELS

*"The angel of the Lord encamps around those who fear Him,
and He delivers them."*　　　　　　(Psalm 34:7)

Let me tell you about something that happened to a five year old and a three year old some years ago... The five year old was sleeping at home in the top bunk when he was awoken by an angel! The angel so was tall that his head reached the ceiling (which was the perfect height for someone in a bunk bed). He was in white with yellow spots. He also had an angel friend who was crouching down talking to the three year old (who was apparently asleep!).

What sort of a conversation they had is a mystery to me, except that the angel said the words "Don't be afraid" when he appeared. Apparently during their chat the angel said that the boy had a good voice and that God would always be with him. When they had finished talking the angels turned and flew out the window!

I've hinted at this before earlier in the book, that we actually live in a spiritual (unseen) dimension as well as the physical one that we can see. Activity in the spiritual dimension affects what we experience in the physical dimension. God is Spirit; He is God and there is none greater than Him. He has an army of angels at His command that He sends as messengers and protectors for those who will know Him. It says in the Bible, *"He makes His angels winds, and His ministers a flame of fire"* and *"Are not all ministering spirits* (angels) *sent out to serve those who are to inherit salvation"* (Hebrews 1:7, 14).

So angels are not mythical creatures like fairies or leprechauns; they are real and servants of God with the purpose to guard us from spiritual attacks and physical danger. Often they are invisible to our eyes, so they will be near and you won't even know it! Occasionally you might be able to sense an angel standing nearby, or to see one. One may even appear with something to say. People in the Bible have had conversations with angels, but it's only because the angel has appeared with a message for them; so it's not right to pray to angels or worship them (Revelation 9:10). Angels are not people who have died, but rather they are powerful spiritual beings created before the earth was made.

You might ask "So if we need protecting, does this mean there is a spiritual enemy too?" Yes. I've already talked about him as someone who tries to put negative thoughts of fear into our minds. The enemy of our souls (the devil) can tempt us to do wrong as well as give us thoughts that are actually lies. However Jesus has given those who know God, the power, words of authority (which the devil must obey) to resist him so that he will flee away.

Did you know we can ask God to surround us with an encampment of angels? Many times when I've woken up fearful at night, I have asked God to send His angels to protect me. Jesus is the commander of the angelic hosts of heaven, so knowing Him comes with many great benefits! Every so often my boys and I go and pray in each room of the house. We each take a wall and ask Jesus to bless the house, to bring peace to the room and for His angels to guard every window and door.

"Those who fear Him," means those who honour, respect and love God. As I'm sure you will notice this kind of fear is one where we are in awe of God, rather than frightened of negative things happening to us.

Maybe you have been having night fears, or get afraid at night time? It is quite natural when the lights are off and our minds begin to imagine things! Yet at the same time God doesn't want you to be afraid.

Shall we pray? *Lord Jesus. I thank You for this house. I ask You to bless this house and to bring peace to my room. Please send Your angels to guard the windows and doors and protect me this night.*

#Day14

SPECIAL DELIVERY

"The angel of the Lord encamps around those who fear Him and He delivers them." (Psalm 34:7)

Have you ever waited in for a parcel and wondered if it was ever going to arrive? You were shopping online with your birthday money last week and finally that new game for your games console is due today! Or maybe you ordered some new clothes or a pair of trainers some days ago and you're hoping they will arrive so that you can wear them to a party that night.

So will it turn up during the morning? You're trying to get on with your day so as not to think about it too much; but then on the other hand you don't want to miss the delivery guy's knock on the door and you really want to see what you ordered! You know some things we have to wait for. Why do we have to wait for stuff? There's a process involved in a delivery. No matter how quickly we want it to arrive it has to be picked off the shelf in the warehouse, packaged, addressed and forwarded to the delivery people. Then the delivery guys have a process all of their own!

We read the words, *"The angel of the Lord encamps around those who fear Him and He delivers them."* It talks about the times when we are in need and feel powerless to get out of our situation on our own. Maybe you've been feeling controlled or intimidated by another person; or perhaps you've got yourself into a mess and you owe people money but you can't pay up. God is able to help you find a way out of those and other situations.

Much like waiting for a delivery, often there's a process that is under way for the rescue plan to unfold, for our rescue to take place. The words *"and He delivers them,"* refer to God's rescue. Psalm 34 was originally written in Hebrew; the word used for "delivers" literally means "to remove." It's a description of how God delivers us. God's rescue plan involves removing us from perilous situations.

In superhero films there's often someone who has been captured and is awaiting rescue. They have no idea of the progress of the plan through which they will be rescued. Maybe the kidnapped person is in a cold cell, hidden from view. Imagine that's you and the Avengers are coming to your aid. You aren't aware of their plans. They could be working out the site of your location, fighting back an evil boss, or flying to your rescue having broken through a blockade. Be encouraged the Lord promises to deliver you as you trust, love and honour Him!

As the battle wages in heaven we know one thing; that the devil is not an equal match for God. For starters God is everywhere, whereas the devil can only be in one place at once. But there is a battle, where the enemy plans destruction and where God sends His angels and intervenes personally to force back those who mean us harm.

When we're thinking about being delivered from a situation it is possible that we have to wait. This doesn't mean God isn't coming to your rescue. His angels are already making an encampment around you. As His child you benefit from His protection.

One of the writers in the Psalms puts it like this, "Put your hope in God, for I will yet praise Him" (Psalm 42:11). What he's saying is that during the time of waiting for rescue, it can be a trial of faith; but he says of God "I will yet praise Him." In other words there will be a time when my deliverance will come. I may have to wait for it, but God will surely come through and I will have cause to celebrate God's rescue.

Shall we pray? Then I have something over the page for you, to help you contemplate these words a bit more... *Father God. I thank You that You are my rescuer. The Bible is full of stories of when you rescued Your people and I know You will do the same for me now. Help me to trust You in the tough times. I know I will praise You for the victory You will give.*

45

PRAYER SPACE

Here's an opportunity to contemplate those words of Psalm 42:11 "Put your hope in God, for I will yet praise Him." As you can see there is some lettering below. Why not use these letters to write out Psalm 42:11 on the opposite page. It's worth putting on some Christian worship music whilst you do this. Be open to God speaking to you through what you do.

Aa Bb Cc Dd
Ee Ff Gg Hh
Ii Jj Kk Ll
Mm Nn Oo Pp
Qq Rr Ss Tt
Uu Vv Ww Xx
Yy Zz

PRAYER SPACE

#Day15

TASTE AND SEE

"Oh, taste and see that the Lord is good!"   (Psalm 34:8)

If you've ever watched those shows like the Bake off, you're probably drawn in by its good humour and great ideas, as well as the bakers themselves; but it's often the thrills and the spills which keep us watching and waiting to see the completed bake. Viewing that Black Forest Gateau or clever Gingerbread house finished to perfection is an awe inspiring sight! It all looks so tasty!

However there's a small drawback to watching the Bake off, especially when your stomach is empty: you can't experience what it tastes like! Just like the cake above; it wasn't just made to look nice, or so that I could draw a picture of it. These things are baked to be tasted.

Sometimes we'll read something about God in the Bible, and forget that this is something to be experienced now! Yes it was written some time ago, but it was all about how God worked in the lives of the people in their day. Now it is your turn. It is your day. To see something without tasting it is not experiencing what it was meant for.

So try it out!

Sometimes the fear of disappointment can hold us back from tasting God's goodness. The cake is laid out in front of us, but we can find it hard to lay aside our worries and enjoy it, because we're being bothered by our fears. God says "Don't be afraid. Choose to trust Me, I have your situation handled. I am your peace." This is the tasting bit, an action you and I have to take. Start by filling up your heart, reminding yourself about who God is. Gain the evidence from God's word and all the times that

God has helped you before and begin to thank God with your speech. Boast in His goodness and let the enemy hear it! Don't put your faith in the voice of fear, but listen to what Jesus says, "Come to me all who are weary and heavy burdened and I will give rest" (Matthew 11:28 NIV).

To taste something is to try it out to see if it's as tasty as it looks; to see if it delivers on what it promises to be. This means letting go of your worries. Ask Jesus to help you with the things you struggle with, then importantly thank God that He is working things out. Thanking when we await God's rescue is speaking in faith, saying "God I put my trust in You even though the outcome is unknown at present, I believe You." That is the tasting part! Putting your confidence in God rather than being afraid of what fear is telling you. God will give you His peace to enjoy. As you do this you will begin to taste God's goodness in the trouble. Remember we said that it's getting into those good habits of reminding ourselves of the truth about God each day.

We have something really incredible offered to us with full permission to enjoy, "Taste and see that the Lord is good." Test out the goodness of God by calling to Him and putting your trust in Him that He will be the answer. We can either believe the lies that our fears tell us, or we can take courage in trusting that God will be good to us. Fear is a bit of an enigma, it can only control us if we believe in it! It can control us and cripple us if we let it; leading to stressing out and missing out on the joy of living.

So really! Try God out! Set your worries aside and place your confidence in God. Taste Him and be at peace.

Father God. I am sorry that I have believed the lies of fear. (Tell Him about what lies you have believed). I believed the lie that I was on my own, and that everything would go wrong. I thank You that You say "Do not be afraid; do not be discouraged, for the Lord your God will be with you wherever you go" (Joshua 1:9). I replace the devil's lies with the truth that I don't have to fear the future because You are with me. I know You look after Your children as a good Father and You look after me.

FINDING REFUGE

"Oh, taste and see that the Lord is good!
Blessed is the man who takes refuge in Him!" (Psalm 34:8)

David would have known about refuge; having been on the run and needing to find somewhere, anywhere safe, to stay protected from the man hunt and preferably a place with not too many eyes watching.

Can you imagine being in David's shoes? Where would *you* look for safety? Would you look for a cave, a forest or a remote dwelling to find rest? Of course a source of water would be essential. To stay one step ahead of your pursuers, you would need to be thinking with the mind of a hunter. Maybe as the hunted you'll be on the look-out for somewhere with an unrestricted view, so you could see your attackers as soon as they reach the horizon. Of course there's some advantage to being hidden as you are able to your see your enemy approaching before they see you. You'll then be able to make quick your escape.

Maybe David found temporary refuge in someone's house; but would he be able to trust those he was staying with? Think of it from the viewpoint of the stranger taking you in. It's an attractive thought to be owed a debt of gratitude by the king; but who to side with? King Saul (the current king of Israel) would certainly reward the person who gave information on a wanted man. The other alternative is to risk being charged with treason by deciding to help David the possible future king!

Now, if you've ever played hide and seek you'll know that it is possible to remain undiscovered for ages by switching places. Of course that's cheating! But people rarely check the same place twice!

We are told in the verses we read that the person who takes refuge in God is blessed (ie. they are happy!). David must have longed for a place that was truly safe. Yet as he thinks about the benefits of a true place of safety, he is reminded that God is the best place to run to when we're overwhelmed or under pressure.

Here God promises to provide peace for you so that you can find rest when you're in the middle of uncertainty. When each day comes with a new challenge and when you don't know how it will go. In the uncertainty God wants you to know that you can trust Him. He is your protector and your lookout. He sees the beginning from the end. He wants us to see things as He sees them. If someone were to tell you that they had been in a time machine and met you 6 months later and that all of the things that you were concerned about turned out for the best for you, I'm sure you would be so relieved! You would probably be less anxious about your present difficulties because you know that they turned out alright. There's no longer that looking over your shoulder wondering when your worries are going catch up with you and bite you on the bum.

God is your refuge, a fortress; your place of certainty in the uncertain.

Remember yesterday we said "Try God out," taste and see that He is good. You might say "I can't have that kind of faith!" Actually you can. Faith comes by hearing and then by doing. You know when we worry we begin processing thoughts in our minds, round and round, picturing the worst-case scenarios that we might have to deal with. How we put faith into practice is to cease the constant thought processing. Instead tell Jesus about your concerns. Ask Him to take care of them; then allow your mind to be at rest. How? Put your confidence in God's ability to protect you from the harm that concerns you.

We said that God tastes good! What good is a cake that is never eaten? When we place our confidence in Him and trust Him with those things that we need, we will experience His goodness. He is a good safe place to come to. Take a look over the page. There's some prayer space for you to share with Jesus your concerns and to receive from Him what you need.

Left Hand

Can you place your left hand on this page and draw around it?
Then whilst talking to God think of the difficulties that you want
to give over to God. Can you write them inside the hand drawing?
(If you don't want to write them why not put in initials instead?).
Then as you pray, thank God that He is your refuge and hand them to Him.

PRAYER SPACE

Right hand

Can you place your right hand on this page and draw around it?
Thank God that you can trust Him when you are having to deal
with uncertain times; why not ask Him for His help and
protection? Then inside your hand drawing, why not write
down what you would like to receive from Him?

THE FEAR OF THE LORD

"Oh, fear the Lord, you His saints,"   (Psalm 34:9)

Imagine you are at home one day and you hear a knock at the door. You get to the door and a basket has been left on your doorstep. As you look at the basket you can see it is well padded and looks like a cosy home for something to snuggle in. You look to see if anyone is around, but they are long gone. So you take a peek inside the basket. To your surprise there's a wee kitten inside! The kitten looks up at you with its big eyes and squeaks.

Well there's nothing to be done but to bring it inside. After a quick search on the internet you discover it needs special milk and a feeding bottle, which you manage to source. Watching the kitten enjoying his first feed with you is a special moment and you decide to keep him.

However after a week or so you slowly begin to realise something about this kitten... that "kitten" is the wrong word for it. A more accurate term would be "cub." Yes this is no domesticated cat; you have taken in a lion! Of course lions require a whole other level of taking care of than a simple house cat. Apart from the size issues and visits you would need to the butchers for feeding time, a lion requires a certain amount of respect that you don't need to give to your common cat. For a start there are safety issues. You may have a bond with the lion which means he may never attack you, but I expect most visitors would not be viewed by the lion in quite the same way. However you look at him, that lion is stronger than you and can pretty much do his own thing if he wants to.

As we've seen, the word "fear" can have a number of meanings. It can be a healthy awareness of danger (such as being in the vicinity of an erupting volcano); but it can also be an unhealthy anxiety of the unknown.

So what does it mean to fear God? It's a bit like our lion scenario. The nature of a lion is that it is strong, powerful and if you have ever heard one roar at close range, your heart will beat much, much, faster! So we give the lion the respect he deserves! To approach a lion without the respect fitting a lion is a very unwise move. Imagine if someone were to give the lion a kick up the bum like some would mistreat a domestic cat; they would be fortunate if they escaped the house with all their limbs!

So when it says *"Oh, fear the Lord, you His saints"* it refers to a healthy respect for who God is. He is the Almighty, our creator. He knows His own mind and as we read in the previous verse, He is only good. Is He safe? Like the lion, He is not safe. So we do well to be on His side! God is love; but He is also holy. This means He is pure and cannot allow evil to get away with its plans in any way. At some point the significance of a crime against another must be brought to light and justice result. We all agree that thieves and murders must face justice. Oh and liars can't be allowed to trick people; and what about bullies who cause so much pain?

The problem is that if you really think about it, we've all done evil in some way. I'm sure you'll agree, like me you've done things wrong that have hurt others, hurt yourself or hurt God. The Bible tells us that these actions separate us from God, showing a lack of fear of Him (Romans 3:23). The good news is that God showed His love in a practical way by paying the fine for a judgement we deserve (Romans 6:23). Like a judge, God will uphold right from wrong, but with the deepest love for you and me, He did what it took to help us avoid the consequences.

Who are His saints? They are those who take up God on His offer to pay our fine. It remains outstanding and unpaid until we do something about it. This is where Jesus comes in. God became man, lived a perfect life and allowed Himself to be unjustly executed as a criminal so that the fallout of our mistakes would be erased. I'd much rather experience God's love than His judgement! If you haven't already accepted His gift, He wants you to take it. That is why He let them put Him on a cross like a common criminal. Over the page is a prayer space to help you to take time to make the most important decision of your life. Why not take a look?

PRAYER SPACE

The Bible tells us that God so loved the world (that is us), that He gave His only Son that whoever believes in Him shall not perish but have everlasting life (John 3:16).

Q - Do you believe that God came to earth for you?
Q - Do you believe that Jesus lived and died for you?
Q - Do you believe that God loves you?

The Bible says that no one is perfect; that we have all done wrong and fallen short of God's standard. Heaven is a perfect place where God is, but we being imperfect are separated from God without Jesus.

Q - Do you admit that you have done wrong?
Q - Are you sorry for those things you have done?
Q - Would you like God to forgive you?

The Bible contains eye witness accounts of how the Romans executed Jesus through the torture of nailing Him to a cross (John 19). God purposed this to happen so that ours wrongs could be erased. He rose from the dead three days later demonstrating that He was God's Son (see John 20).

Q – Do you believe Jesus was God's only Son?
Q – Do you believe that He died for you?
Q – Do you believe He rose from the dead?

Jesus said "Whoever wants to become my disciple must deny themselves and take up their cross and follow me." (Matthew 16:24).

Q – Will you receive God's free gift of wrongs forgiven and eternal life with Him in heaven?
Q – Do you choose to live your life for Jesus?

PRAYER SPACE

Whether you've been to church loads of times or never set foot inside a church, God wants you to know Him. When you pray this prayer something will happen. God will come close to you whether you sense Him close or not. He wants you to know that you are His forever!

If you have chosen to follow Jesus, please pray this prayer...

> *Dear Lord God; Almighty God, I come to You as a stranger, but I want to be Your friend.*
>
> *I know that in Your deep love for me You welcome me. Thank You for sending Jesus into the world to show me what You are like. I believe He is Your Son and that He lived on this earth and that He was executed by the Romans. Thank You that You planned this in order that I could be made free; free from the power of the enemy over my life and free to be forgiven for all of my wrongs.*
>
> *I believe Jesus rose from the dead and that I can know Him with me every day.*
>
> *Please forgive me for all the wrong things that I have done. I am truly sorry. In respect for You, I turn away from the wrong things I have done and choose to follow You. Help me to live my life for You.*
>
> *Now I ask You to come and take over my heart and my life. In Jesus' name!*

Once you have taken this step with God, the Bible calls you a child of God *"Yet to all who did receive Him, to those who believed in His name, He gave the right to become children of God"* (John 1:12). This means that you have peace with God; and God as the best loving Father includes you in His family and will guide you in life, protect you and provide for the things you need. This is the start of a wonderful friendship with God!

#Day18

WITH A CHILD'S EYES

"Oh, fear the Lord, you His saints,
for those who fear Him have no lack!"   (Psalm 34:9)

Christmas time at the age of 8 years old was a very exciting time in my life. We lived out in the country and there was plenty of activity making decorations at school and rehearsals at church in the run up to Christmas. I remember being a shepherd in the church nativity and singing "Little donkey" with my class in the school play. You never forget those magical moments like opening the advent calendar door to discover a mini toy animal inside; and of course there were the presents... things that I hoped for, but had no idea what would actually be beneath the wrapping paper. Dad was a Pastor of a church and money was tight. Little did I know it at the time, but my folks were struggling to find money for presents.

Christmas day came around and I had placed the largest sock I could find at the bottom of my bed. When I woke it was filled with all sorts of mini presents! When everyone was up, we made our way downstairs to discover a snooker table! Wrapped presents were there for us including a watch with a space invaders game on it! Christmas was a wonderful time which we all enjoyed so much. Apparently, all this turned out to be quite last minute. I found out years later that my dad was given some money a few days before Christmas and mum and dad knew just how to use it!

We read the words *"for those who fear Him have no lack."* We saw yesterday that rather than being frightened, the kind of fear that relates to God is a healthy fear, because He is totally good. There is no evil in Him whatsoever. So fearing the Lord is a deep love and respect of who He is, where no harm will come to us and where there is a supply that He provides for us that won't run out.

You know as little children we look to our parents and we believe in them without question. To the young mind there is no problem too big that mum or dad can't sort out. As a child we know our folks will look after us and we look to them innocently expecting to be fed and be safe, as well as giving us gifts. To us they appear super human. As we grow up we lose something of that expectation as we learn more of what our parents have to deal with. More and more we begin to realise that our parents are human and now as a parent myself I can tell you I am not super human!

However when it comes to God, He wants you to view Him in this way: as if you had the trust of a little child. He wants you to come to Him with the expectation that you would for the best dad in the world; a dad who loves you, who would never harm you in any way and who would lay down his life for you. Jesus said that actually we cannot enter His world without seeing God like this. He said *"Let the little children come to me, and do not hinder them, for the kingdom of God belongs to such as these. Truly I tell you, anyone who will not receive the kingdom of God like a little child will never enter it."* (Luke 18:17). Jesus also said *"I praise you, Father, Lord of heaven and earth, because You have hidden these things from the wise and learned, and revealed them to little children"* (Luke 10:21).

There is a secret door into His world that God wants you to discover. He wants you to understand how the Kingdom of heaven works. It begins with a childlike trust that wholeheartedly trusts Father God for the solution. So look to God for the answer; see that you are a child in His house. You have access to the riches of heaven's storehouse!

Ask Him to deal with the things you can't, open your hands out to God and pass to Him your worries. In your heart and mind choose to ignore the whispers of fear.

Let your mind be at peace as you choose to trust that Father God is working on your difficulties. Believe it when God says to you that you will not lack what you need; He loves to give good gifts! Over the page is a prayer space for you to ask God to show you what His world is like.

PRAYER SPACE

Take a quick look at the picture on page 58. Not the finest drawing you'll ever see! But let me quickly tell you about this picture. Years ago I was worshipping God and He put this thought in my mind saying that I was to look at Him with the eyes of a child and this picture popped into my head. I quickly scribbled it down and to me when I look at it, it encourages my faith and reminds me that I am a child in God's house with access to His riches as I trust Him like a child trusts a good father.

Sometimes God will put a picture into your mind about what He is like. You might not be the best at drawing, it doesn't matter. Draw it anyway. It is communicating a precious concept that God is speaking to you, and it will encourage you as you look back at it.

So in this space just below here I want you to draw a door.

Have you drawn the door above? Now look at the door, then close your eyes and ask Jesus to take you through the door to show you something of Him and His kingdom. Imagine you are walking through the door with Jesus and draw on the opposite page what comes to mind. Then try and understand what God might be saying to you. He will tell you something that agrees with the words and concepts of the Bible.

PRAYER SPACE

#Day19

ACTUAL REALITY

"The young lions suffer want and hunger;
but those who seek the Lord lack no good thing." (Psalm 34:10)

Have you ever tried out those virtual reality headsets? You know the ones, they are linked up to a games console and you put the headset over your eyes and you are suddenly in another world? Well, a while back I tried out a Star Wars game on a VR headset and it was amazing. I was in front of an enormous monster (the Rancor!) and as I turned my head to the left and moved it was like I was in a new world (a scary world where I was about to get eaten!). It was like I had been teleported into a real life Star Wars film!

As soon as I took the headset off, I was back in the shop with people staring at me like I was some sort of weirdo.

Jesus spoke about the Kingdom of heaven; a dimension, a world that exists beyond this world that that we can experience and see. You could compare it to that virtual reality game in a way; although the Star Wars game is another world you can step into, it only exists on a games console and when you're done all you get is a dizzy head. However, Jesus spoke about a real kingdom; a spiritual realm that impacts this one and can make a difference in our lives today. He talked about the kingdom of heaven quite a bit, telling us about it and how it works. He would say *"It is like a mustard seed, which a man took and sowed in the ground"* (Matthew 13:31). He also compared His kingdom to a hidden treasure, a pearl of great price, indicating its value for those who take a hold of it.

Today we read *"The young lions suffer want and hunger; but those who seek the Lord lack no good thing."* What does that mean? The term "young lions" has a double meaning. First the obvious: if you've ever seen those wildlife programmes you will see that a young lion is strong, fast and therefore is excellent at getting it's kill for food. You would always expect a young lion to catch what it needed.

The second meaning was probably a term people of the day used for the rich. You wouldn't ever expect rich people to run out of their supply. Do you get what its saying? Even those who are rich and depend on their vast wealth are less secure than you whom God says will lack no good thing!

You might remember that we read this yesterday, "Those who fear the Lord have no lack." Isn't this just a repetition of the previous verse? YES!! And there is a reason for it! It's quite significant when we discover words or phrases repeated in the Bible. In Hebrew when an idea is repeated, it's like it has been written in BLOCK CAPTIALS or underlined. It's as if God is saying "If you missed it the first time, I'll say it again, so that you see that I mean it!" Okay, so we get that it's important.

Here's the bit you need to get… The difference is the source of the supply. A big store of riches might seem a lot, but things can happen to impact this and what seemed as security has all gone. Rich people can go bankrupt; but those who love and seek first God and His kingdom (Matthew 6:33) have access to a supply that won't run out. You have access to God's world that you can step into at any time. His kingdom has an infinite supply. So you might not have it all piled up in gold coins in front of you, but if you were to compare the two of what is accessible to you and what the rich have at their disposal, the difference is that yours will not run out!

So the big question is then, how do we access God's kingdom supply? It says "Those who seek the Lord" won't go without. Continue what you have been doing as you've been reading this book. The prayer spaces are there to help you to seek God. As you look to Him, depend on Him and trust Him that He will help you with the things you can't do, He will make sure that you have what you need and more besides! Don't put your faith in your fears, discover the evidence of what He is like and rely on Him.

AN INVITATION

"Come, O children, listen to me;"   (Psalm 34:11)

Years ago my younger brother Andy's birthday was just around the corner, so I thought I'd sort him out a really special gift. Like my older brother, Andy is also an Arsenal supporter. Well, the footballer Paul Merson had just published a book about his life, so I decided to find out where his book was being sold and if the footballer was doing a book signing. What a great gift to have a signed copy of a book by your footballing hero! So the day came around and I joined the lengthy queue, people wearing Arsenal tops were clutching copies of the book. It took a while, but as I neared the Arsenal and England Midfielder I was feeling quite excited.

Finally I made it to the front of the queue to see Paul Merson sitting there. As I handed him the book he smiled at me and said "Hello," and I asked him if he could write "To Andy, Happy birthday," which I think that was what he wrote and we said "Goodbye." It was only a brief meeting and quite uneventful, but one I'll never forget. To be close to someone you admire like that is an incredible feeling.

What about you? Can you think of someone you really admire? A sports star, an actor, maybe a preacher, or someone involved in local policing; what about a nurse who works in a hospital? A hero you have seen and look up to (even a family member). Now have a think about what it is like to see someone who you admire. There you are in a room at a gathering and they see you and call you over. I expect you are feeling relaxed and happy in their company. You feel honoured that this person wants you to be with them and it's a delight to be in their presence.

In the bit that we just read, we saw the words *"Come, O children, listen to me."* It's easy to read and totally miss what God is saying, since the words "Listen to me" tend to jump out and immediately we go to instruction mode thinking "Okay God wants me to listen to Him." Yes those words are important, but only when understood with the rest of it. Okay, what did we miss? First God, the Creator of the universe is actually inviting us into a relationship. He is welcoming us to be where He is. First He wants us to seek Him, to come close to Him, as His son or daughter to understand what He is like, to be in conversation with Him.

You are invited by Father God to come close to Him; today, now. He actually wants to be with you! He's calling you over and asking you to spend time with Him. He's interested in you and all that is going on in your life. Just like the best loving Father who wants you to succeed in life and do the good things that you love to do; nothing brings a good father more joy than knowing that you are enjoying life. So when you talk to Him, just wait for a moment, be aware that He is present with you, He is for you not against you.

Do you know that it's easier to listen to the advice of a person that we have respect for and admire? Their words take on so much more meaning because we know where they are coming from. I am more likely to take footballing tips from Paul Merson, than I am from some random guy that I might meet in the football stand. God wants to speak to you.

Why not ask Him something now as He wants you to listen to Him. Why not ask Him to tell you what He thinks of you? What good thought comes to mind? God often uses our thoughts to speak to us, so being sensitive to what He is saying requires that we switch off from all distractions and wait for something to come to mind, it doesn't take long. Did something pop into your head? Maybe it was a picture?

Go ahead, ask Him what it means and see if He gives you more understanding about it. If it is something good it most probably is God. To listen is to take notice of what is said. Take notice that God loves you and has good things in store for you as you trust Him.

FOLLOWING HIS WAYS

"Come, O children, listen to me;
*   I will teach you the fear of the Lord."*   (Psalm 34:11)

The other day I was in unfamiliar territory and needed to find a shop. Being on foot in the rain wasn't so nice, so the maps app was going to come in very handy. My wife put in the shop name and it told us we had an 8 minute walk. So off we headed hoping that we'd be able to get out of that cold rain super quickly. Five minutes (and one big hill) later, I asked Debs if we were nearly there as our location didn't seem to correspond with our destination! So we checked her phone only to find out that it was telling us we now had 13 minutes to go!

Unable to believe what the phone was telling us we checked everything and realised we'd taken a wrong turn. It was actually right at the start where the SAT NAV told us to "Head south," and we (without the benefit of a compass) headed north. You would hope that after a few steps the SAT NAV would realise our error and tell us "Turn around where possible," but it didn't because we were walking. Instead it just re-routed us around the block, the long way up the hill in the rain!

If we're to make the right progress on this journey of life, it's important to set off in the right direction. Some people don't recognise God as the authority in their lives and although He is saying "Go this way," they would quite like His guidance for life decisions, but not to tell them what not to do. The trouble is that both knowing what the right life choice is and how to live morally is actually more inter-connected than some think. Take the example of the person who tells lies to cover up mistakes they have made; honesty will always open doors that double-dealing never will.

When we try and live our own way with God just "on the side" to help point us in the right direction, much like the SAT NAV situation that I had; we'll find we're likely to be directed the long hard way round where our character is shaped and we learn we need God more than we think!

You see God is a good God and He wants His people to be like Him. We become more like a person the more we spend time with them. We also understand their ways, what they like and what pushes them away. Life can have its detours that can be avoided when we spend time listening to His ways. As we've seen before "The fear of the Lord," is the respect of who God is (the Lord Almighty) and submitting to Him as the authority over what we say and do, as well as what choices we make.

This brings me to one of those "What if" questions that young people can sometimes wrestle with... What if I make the wrong choice? This could relate to choosing subjects at school, whether or not to date a particular person, or it could be your folks have split up and you are having to make some tricky decisions. Maybe you feel a pressure to know what you should do when you feel you just don't have a clue?

You know following God's guidance is a bit like a jigsaw puzzle. There are loads of pieces that fit together, but there's no way you can know how it all fits together immediately. It takes time examining different decisions, like pieces of the puzzle before choosing one. If you are following Jesus, talking to Him about your future and honouring His ways (not perfection!) and you have a choice where you can't decide, just pick one. If it's the wrong one Jesus will make sure things don't go wrong. He will either stop that opportunity from happening or bring about something that is 100 times better. God guides us by telling us stuff, but He will also guide you through your circumstances, catching you so you won't fall. Don't fear! You can trust Him!

Over the page is a prayer space with loads of jigsaw puzzle pieces. Begin by thanking God that He is working in your life and on your behalf and ask Him to reveal to you pieces of the puzzle of your life that will help you to make good choices for future decisions.

PRAYER SPACE

As you pray ask God about the things named on the puzzle pieces; then write around the puzzle pieces what you feel the answers are at this point in your life. Maybe there's puzzle pieces you'd like to add?

#Day22

GOOD FOUNDATIONS

"What man is there who desires life and loves many days,
that he may see good?"   (Psalm 34:12)

If you were to build a house, what do you think is the most important part of it? Which part would you spend the most time getting right? Would it be the roof, since it keeps the rain off? What about the doors to keep your property secure? Could it be the luxury fittings, heating or a nice soft carpet? If you asked an expert, he or she would say that the foundations are the most important part of any build. This base to the house has to be as solid as a rock, since the foundations underpin everything that goes on top of it. If the foundations are not secure, the house could fall on top of you at any moment. Everything in a house depends on there being a good foundation built.

Did you know that it takes a similar amount of time to put in the foundations as it does to build up the walls? A builder will dig deep troughs into the ground about the depth of a person, lined up in relation to the footprint and dimensions of the building. The builder then mixes a load of concrete with a large mixing lorry and tips the concrete into those troughs in stages until they are filled up. Once set, he will then pour more concrete over as a thick layer on top to create the base. This needs to set properly before any walls can be built on it. It takes the same amount of time to then do the walls.

So foundations are very important. In the bit we read David is about to give us some God-given advice for living; so he says, *"What man is there who desires life and loves many days, that he may see good?"* I'm sure every one of us wants to live life to the full, to love, to be free to do a job that makes the most of our abilities, to not die young and have a good life.

If this is what we desire, we will see God's goodness in our lives only when we are building on a solid foundation. Imagine if the builder didn't dig down deep enough, or got the mix of concrete wrong. After a while of living in the house, cracks will begin to appear in the walls, ones that get bigger and bigger. It could be the most beautiful house with all the fancy furnishings; but if it has a poor foundation, the house is unsafe and all that has been invested into it could be destroyed if a storm were to hit.

Jesus once compared a house build to the kind of teaching that we decide to put into practice each day of our lives. Every one of us is living our lives according to a certain standard. So a person living by their own standards just doing what they want to do, might have no problem with being mean to that kid at school that is different from them.

Jesus has another standard of living; one that honours God's ways, one that resists doing evil, that trusts God in the tough times and that puts Him as number 1. What you believe about life, how it came about and who you have decided Jesus is, will affect the foundation of what you build your life on. Jesus said *"Therefore everyone who hears these words of mine and puts them into practice is like a wise man who built his house on the rock. The rain came down, the streams rose, and the winds blew and beat against that house; yet it did not fall because it had its foundations on the rock"* (Matt 7:24-27).

As you read on tomorrow, God is about to give you His Maker's instructions on how to build your life. Some of it will take some discipline, as doing the right thing is not always easy; but it's the way He calls us to live. There are great rewards for living God's way. You will love life and see His goodness working in your life every day; also those liars "fear" and "anxiety" will struggle more and more to get a hold on your life. Don't forget that in putting God's words into practice you remain devoted to Him. Doing these things without a love for God will be very hard going!

Over the page is a prayer space to help you to consider the areas of your life and to what amount they are built on the foundations of God's words.

PRAYER SPACE

Below is a list of rooms for you to consider how much you are allowing God in to build in those areas of your life. Why not pray about each room and write or draw in the house opposite what ways you are letting God into those spaces, or how God is saying He wants you to let Him in.

HALL – Where people are invited in

What truly trustworthy friends do you have?
Do your friends influence you for good or for bad? Or do you influence them?
Who do you spend a lot of time with?
Is God welcome in your home?

KITCHEN/DINER – Where food is prepared for the family and eaten

Jesus was a servant to others. In what way do you serve others?
What sort of "spiritual food" (Bible stuff) do you eat that makes you strong?
Do you spend time slowly reading and thinking about God's words?
Or do you rush through and forget you even read the Bible?
Do you need to stop taking on board any spiritual things which aren't from God?

LOUNGE – Where leisure takes place

How much of your free time is spent using a screen?
How do you feel in yourself after using a screen?
Does using social media affect your mental health?
Would it be healthy to rethink this area?
What social activities are you involved in?
Can you do something active outside to unwind?
Are you in a church youth group?

BEDROOM – A place of rest, dreaming and homework

Do you allow God into your private space?
Do you tell God about your hopes and dreams and listen for His?
Do you ask God for His inspiration before doing your homework?

BATHROOM – To wash and cleanse

How do you deal with those negative things we all pick up from the day?
Do you come to God regularly to ask to be forgiven for wrongs you have done?
Do you regularly forgive those who have done wrong to you?
Do you receive His forgiveness and go with joy believing you are forgiven?

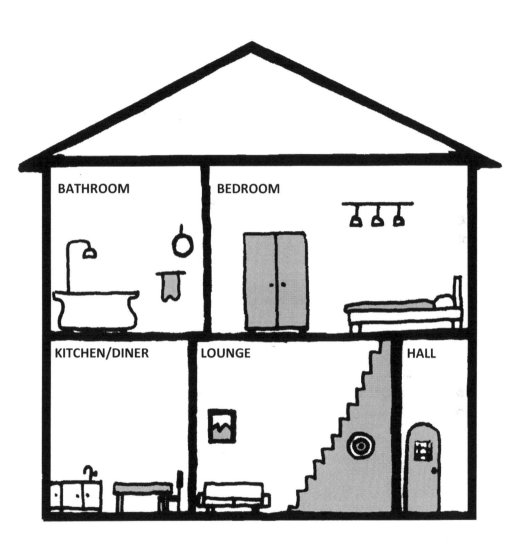

THE WORDS OF OUR MOUTHS

"Keep your tongue from evil"   (Psalm 34:13)

Some of the words people say can be very catchy. A person only has to say them once or twice; and not only have we remembered them, but unknowingly we end up believing them. When I was five or six years old I can still remember a girl saying these words in the school playground, "Sticks and stones may break my bones, but words will never hurt me." No, she wasn't being beaten by sticks or pelted with stones; someone had called her a nasty name. Her defence was to say that she wasn't hurt by negative words in the same way that physical pain can bring hurt.

Unfortunately the fact is, negative words that people say to us or the names they label us with, often do affect us more than we think. Even though we might try to forget the negative things that are said to us, sometimes our minds register these things on a much deeper level. Subconsciously our brains process what has been said and maybe we even believe it. Now obviously if someone has something negative to say to us which is true, this can help us. You know, constructive criticism, where a teacher might tell a pupil he is being lazy with his homework and needs to put in more effort, which the pupil knows is true because they completed an hour's task in five minutes.

But then there are the words that really aren't helpful, that bring people down and hurt them inside. A person might ask, "How can my words be evil?" Say for example you said to someone, "Hey, did you realise that you have an ugly nose." You might just be joking and just trying to have some banter, but to the person hearing it, they may go home and examine their nose in the mirror. Then (and this is the evil bit), the enemy flies on the back of what you have said and whispers in that person's ear, "Your nose makes you look ugly." The enemy uses our words to speak his lies into people's hearts to make a person unhappy and lead them into more negative behaviours. Imagine the person believes these lies that the enemy has whispered to them. What then if they are invited to a party, but having no self-confidence either turns down the invite, or does go but doesn't enjoy themselves because they hate the way they look.

No one would want to be the mouthpiece for evil, but that is how easily it is done, because our words have the power to enslave people, and the enemy is ready to exploit them. But you know what, as a child of God your words also have the power to set people free. When we speak an encouraging word to someone that is true, the reverse happens.

What if you see someone at school that walks past you every day, but you just notice how they always look really down. A negative thing would be to say "Cheer up misery guts," and could do quite a bit of harm; however what if you were to ask God in your heart, "What do you love about that person?" Something might come in to your mind. The Holy Spirit might draw to your attention something about that person's appearance. It could be that they have beautiful eyes, or that they look like a really kind person and you can tell them that. Alternatively God might speak to you and put a thought in your heart like, "Tell that person 'I felt God whispered in my ear that you were born for greatness,' you're a born leader." Imagine how that truth might encourage that person to see themselves and their future with hope, rather than despair.

We read yesterday that God wants to build good foundations in our lives and our speech is one of those things that He wants us to hand over to Him. This means that when a harsh or negative word is on the tip of our tongue, we stop ourselves from saying it to someone. Instead we look at them through God's eyes and ask Him, "What do you love about that person?" I'd much rather serve God's purposes than the devil's.

Shall we pray? *Father God. I'm sorry for the times I have used negative words that have hurt others. I would much rather people were better off after seeing me than worse off. Would You show me how I can speak Your encouraging words to others? In Jesus' name!*

SPEAKING THE RIGHT LANGUAGE

"Keep your tongue from evil

and your lips from speaking deceit." (Psalm 34:13)

Have you ever been in a country where they speak a different language from the one you are used to? Communicating in the language of the nation you are visiting is really the only way to get things done like saying "Hello," buying a croissant, or finding out where the toilets are.

Years ago I took a 10 week crash course in speaking Russian as I was going on a mission trip. I must say it was super-tricky. For a start, they use letters like these… Русский …this word is pronounced "Roos-key" and is actually the word "Russian" in Russian. So you can imagine how much my brain hurt just trying to learn how to say stuff.

At the end of my 10 weeks I was able to greet people both in the morning and evening, I could say please and thank you, order a coffee (and cakey), ask for and understand directions, as well as learning some cultural dos and don'ts. I expect I was able to understand travel and bits like that too. So I felt I at least had made the effort to communicate with the locals, rather than just speaking slower or louder in English with hand gestures.

What was my time like in Russia? Well I wasn't actually going to Russia. Did I travel through Russian then? No I went to Estonia. Estonia is one of the Baltic States that used to be a part of Russia; however they gained independence through a grim time of conflict where many lives were lost. When I got to Estonia I quickly discovered that they no longer spoke Russian. They actually had their own language now (Estonian) and to speak Russian was culturally insensitive!!

As those who follow Jesus, we are called to speak the language of His Kingdom wherever we go. What am I talking about? The language of truth. The bit we read said, *"What man is there who desires life and loves many days, that he may see good? Keep your tongue from evil and your lips from speaking deceit."* Deceit is deception; in other words lies or tricking people; and this is what God wants us to stay away from.

You know there are different forms of lies. There's the half-truth, where someone is asked a question and answers whilst keeping part of the truth secret. A parent might ask their son, "Were you late home from school today?" The son was serving a detention, but to provide a cover story he went to his friend's house for two minutes. "Oh yes" he replies, "I was at Sam's house." A half-truth is deception. It's not the language of heaven. What about "white lies," where a person promises to send an email and forgets about it. Then when asked says "I sent it you a few days ago, have you checked your spam folder?" knowing full well that they didn't send the email in the first place! Then there's exaggeration of a story. Maybe a girl caught a glimpse of a film star whilst on an outing in London, but in the retelling of the story turns it into a conversation and a phone number!

Telling the truth is the language of God's kingdom, the language of heaven. We have seen that harmful fears (that don't protect us from danger) are actually lies. For the truth of God to grow in our hearts we have to stay away from producing words that deceive others. The more we speak truth, the more we will realise that we are speaking God's language which will help us to identify lies easier too. The Bible tells us that the truth sets us free (John 8:32). This means that there will be times when you will be challenged to tell the truth, even though it may be difficult to do. This is building on the strong foundation of God's word and by following God's ways you will see His goodness breaking out in your life.

Time to take all this to God! *Father God. I thank You that You are the true and Living God. You are faithful and I know I can always trust Your words and promises. Please cause me to identify the lies that deceive and help me to speak out the words and language of Your Kingdom. In Jesus' name!*

#Day25

FACING THE RIGHT DIRECTION

"Turn away from evil and do good,"   (Psalm 34:14)

What's your heart searching for? A good place to discover what that might be is to call up the search history on your phone. This might have some clues as to those things your heart is going after. I expect you'll find in there plenty of homework related research in that search history! Perhaps it might include searches for answers to those tricky questions like "What is the fastest skin care product at removing spots?" Maybe the list contains links to eBay for products that you'd like for Christmas or birthday?   What about social networking sites as you spend time connecting with friends or watching those funny cat videos?

You see we are heart driven people, moved in a certain direction by our inner desires, just like when we go to a shopping mall. If you are anything like me, you will only spend time in those shops that interest you. The heart motivates and directs us. Unfortunately, the enemy has worked this out and believes that if he can capture our hearts, he can affect our thoughts and therefore influence what we do and say in a negative way.

We read the words *"Turn away from evil and do good;"* words that appeal to the heart to be motivated towards goodness rather than evil. So it's really important if negative emotions attack your heart that you don't get directed towards evil or destructive actions. What sort of things do we get motivated to do when we're feeling down, angry or frustrated? Could it be turning to look at negative images online? Most if not all of those types of images will be lies, motivated by evil, filtered and edited to represent a fake situation as if it were a true story. Viewing them can get you addicted. This is not who you are, you don't have to let this stuff control you; but you have to want to be free from its grip! Maybe you feel the urge to harm yourself? Again the enemy will entice you to think it will help you, but Jesus wants you to be free from the control of such things, as they will leave you feeling empty and sore. You are loved and of priceless worth to Jesus.

How do I turn from evil that is attacking my mind? What do I do when I feel the enemy is trying to pull me into some negative behaviour? At times it can feel like evil is knocking on the door of your heart. Firstly I recognise that I have to do something about it. Doing nothing to resist it often leads to submitting to it. I talk to Jesus and tell him that the devil is knocking on my door and ask Him to go answer it. Imagine the shock when the devil sees Jesus standing there, not willing to let him in!

Often that is enough to reject the pull of evil to a negative behaviour, but sometimes tempting thoughts persist. Jesus wants us to win. So secondly I recognise that I need to turn away from those nagging thoughts. This might mean leaving the room, or the person/people (if their words or actions are the unhelpful thing taking place), or switching off a device. If I am alone and tempted I might read a book to distract me, but I find the most helpful thing is to put on a worship song. As soon as I begin to think on and verbalise the words that I hear it turns my desires back to Jesus and away from the negative things trying to make their way into my heart.

Did you know that if a bad thought comes into your mind, that is not a sin? Rather, it depends what you do with that thought that determines if you sin or not. Say for example you're in a shop and someone suggests that you steal a Mars bar as no one is about, you didn't come up with that thought; but what you decide to do next depends whether you do wrong or not. In the same way, the enemy can place negative thoughts in our mind, thoughts that we didn't come up with. It is what we do with that thought that turns to sin or not. You actually have the power to reject a bad thought that comes into your mind as the Bible says that those who are in Christ are no longer slaves to sin (Galatians 4:7). You and I have a new Master, Jesus, who wants us to be free from the control of sin and wrong thoughts. Jesus has set you free. The evidence is over the page...

WHO AM I?

Take a look at these pictures and maybe look up some of the Bible verses to remind you how loved, beautiful, gifted and wanted you are.

You are SIGNIFICANT, ACCEPTED and SECURE in Christ.

CHASING PEACE

"Turn away from evil and do good;
seek peace and pursue it." (Psalm 34:14)

Have you ever been around people who are constantly having disputes with others? You know the type; put them in an empty room with a mirror and before you know it they've started an argument. Maybe you can think of someone like that? Maybe that's you??!!

King Saul was a man who was prone to rages. This was how he got to know David before the Goliath victory (1 Samuel 15:14-35). Whenever Saul became tormented by his thoughts, he would become difficult to be around. Saul's servants suggested a skilful musician might calm Saul's mind and they recommended David. As a boy David would worship God on the lyre and this is what would calm Saul's anger. Now much later after David's victory against Goliath (and many other victories later) King Saul was now pursuing David with a rage that would not be cooled.

Anger is one of those emotions with both positive and negative sides. God is said to get angry at the injustices of this world. Such anger can motivate us to take action when we see wrongs that are being overlooked by governments or large organisations. Anger directed in the right way can lead to incredible change that can affect many lives for good. However, much of the time anger is not used to bring about positive outcomes.

Take for example road rage. All drivers have to follow the rules of the road to provide safety for pedestrians, cyclists and other road users. Unfortunately if someone makes a mistake without noticing those around them, it is likely to provoke a response of anger. I used to be like this when I was a younger driver. I would be this kind polite person who was nice to be around, but then put me in a car and I'd be yelling at other drivers calling them names and allsorts. I'm not like that anymore!

Over the last few days we've been reading about following God's ways. What are those ways that will lead to the promise of fulfilled lives? Firstly it's our words; avoiding speaking negative words, instead saying good things to others using heaven's language of truth. Secondly we looked at turning from negative behaviours and discovering who we are in Christ.

Much like temptation, we have a choice when anger rises in our hearts. It's powerful and often we can feel like wanting to punch something. The trouble with anger is that it doesn't tell us the whole story. It associates with having been wronged and the need to deal with a situation, but it doesn't always help with how to resolve the situation. Often anger is visible. When others see it, they know that something is wrong. This is the point where controlling that anger will enable you to find the solution to the cause of your anger. We read the words *"Seek peace and pursue it"* encouraging us not to take revenge, escalating the problem, but rather to recognise that steps need to be taken to deal with it.

God loves to give us wisdom when we're open to listening to what He has to say. Did you know there is a big difference between "peace keeping" and "peace making"? Peace keeping is all about making everybody happy and avoiding arguments. This is not what it means when it says "seek peace." Rather we have the more difficult task of peace making. Peace making is about facing everyone up to the problem and confronting the issue in order that the future for all involved is a harmonious one.

Sometimes you might need to talk to someone you trust about what is making you angry. Getting someone's advice can enable you to think through the options and best decide what to do. Maybe you don't even know what is making you angry? There are a lot of confusing emotions that occur in your teen-age years. Let's chat to God about this...

Father God. I thank You that You made me and that You understand me. You know what is going on in my mind and how I have these powerful emotions raging inside of me. Thank You for being Yahweh Shalom "I am the Lord your peace." Thank You that You calm the storm. As I walk into Your presence right now, please cause my heart to be still. In Jesus' name.

ACCESS TO THE THRONE ROOM

"The eyes of the Lord are toward the righteous"   (Psalm 34:15)

I wonder what would happen if the Queen of England were to announce on TV that if anyone wanted to pop in for a cuppa to say "Hello," that "one's door was always open"? I expect within minutes (after checking that it wasn't April fool's day) a steady stream of people would be found queuing up at the doors of Buckingham Palace. That queue would most probably grow to become a crowd, multiplying hour upon hour until eventually causing road closures and diversions in the surrounding area.

Kings and Queens are notably difficult to meet up with for a chat, simply because of who they are. Aside from riches, they hold the position and responsibilities of leadership for their nation, so it wouldn't be right for just anyone to be able to call them up wanting a piece of their time to ask for stuff. Those who do find themselves having an audience with royalty are normally there because they deserve it, invited because of something remarkable they've done, such as achieving the world record for the highest stack of pancakes (okay, maybe something more sensible!).

Some people see God's accessibility as being a bit like meeting a king. Even though they are a Christian they don't feel deserving enough to enter God's presence because of something they've done which keeps them from talking to Him. In their minds it's only the "good Christians" that see powerful things happen. You might remember two days ago we had a prayer space with Bible verses stating just who you are in Christ. It states that all who know Jesus can freely come into God's throne room because of what Jesus has done for us. It is Jesus who makes us righteous.

What does this word "righteous" mean? It means being "right with God" being free from guilt or wrongdoing. Our guilt keeps us from God's presence, but Jesus death and resurrection cancels out our guilt and brings us back to God.

As we begin the Christian life we discover that we are only forgiven because of what Jesus has done. We receive His forgiving love and our sins are wiped out. Yet after a while some start to think "Right, now it's up to me to keep it up." Let me tell you that this is wrong thinking! The only thing you have to keep up is a right relationship with Jesus. All other righteous deeds will follow by His power! We become righteous because of what Jesus has done; no special deeds deserving merit are required to come close to God! It is only Jesus who makes it possible for us to access God's throne. Access to a seat in the King's throne room means that when you pray it has real power. God will command His angels concerning you because you have asked or spoken His words believing.

There are some incredible verses in Ephesians 2:6-7 that say God has, *"...**seated us with Him in heavenly places in Christ Jesus**, so that in the coming ages He might show the immeasurable riches of His grace in His kindness toward us in Christ Jesus."*

I wonder what it would have been like to sit on the throne of a real king or queen in days gone by? Just imagine the power they would have been able to wield, simply by speaking a word. Once a directive was made by a king it had to be implemented. We call this authority, when someone has both the position and the power by which their commands are actioned. Jesus' righteousness positions you in a place of authority near heaven's throne where God is. This is what it means to be seated in heavenly places, with permission into God's throne room where there is even a seat for us to access heaven's resources whenever we pray! The Psalm says *"the eyes of the Lord are toward the righteous."* His eyes are toward the righteous, that's you! You have access to His riches and authority to speak His words where powerful prayer is needed to bring about change.

Lord Jesus. Thank You that I am righteous because of You. You are the King upon the throne, thank You that I have access to Your throne room. In Jesus' name I command anger and negative fears to be gone!

A CRY FOR HELP

"The eyes of the Lord are toward the righteous
and His ears toward their cry."   (Psalm 34:15)

A while back we had a family outing where we found ourselves at the Peace Maze in Northern Ireland. As one of the world's largest hedge mazes, we thought it would be fun to do with the boys and their cousins.

As we approached the maze entrance the thought came to mind that it might be worth having a strategy before we went in. The last thing we wanted was to end up lost and confused wandering through the maze for hours 'til it was dark. Unfortunately, before I had a chance to voice my concerns, the boys and their cousins were off running into the maze in different directions. I found myself calling after them "Stay together!!" Hardly an effective strategy, but better than nothing! At this point the maze was now doubly hard, we had to get through the maze as well as find the boys. "Yey, it'll be fun they said..." Hmmm... famous last words?

Eventually we adults reached what looked to be the halfway point, a bridge that enables you to see above the maze (but not high enough to see sons or nephews!). At this point we had been there a while and it was getting time we completed the maze. I began calling out the names of my boys, but to no response. I called out in different directions in case my voice was being carried by the wind; but I heard nothing back, not even the faint sound of children playing. I began to wonder "Why is it that they haven't called back to me? At what point does a parent begin to actually get concerned that they have lost their children in a maze?"

Then, when my stress levels were getting particularly high, I saw one of them burst through a gap in a hedge deeper into the maze. I called out to them saying that we all needed to get going. From my vantage point I would be able to quickly direct them to us, but as quickly as I saw them, they had disappeared. "Was I being heard?" I thought to myself. Surely everyone within a 10 mile radius had heard me calling out. Then, in a matter of minutes the boys suddenly all appeared on the bridge and we were able to progress through the maze together.

But I had a burning question that I had to ask my son as we continued through the maze. "Did you hear me calling your name?" I asked. He replied, "Yes I heard you dad, I went to get Ben so we could find you." My next question of equal importance was "Why didn't you call back to me, so that I knew you had heard me?? We thought you were gone from the maze!!" His response was that he wasn't ignoring me, but that he was trying to get over to where I was.

We read the words, *"...His ears toward their cry."* Have you ever wondered if God has heard you calling His name? The word "cry" is less to do with tears and more to do with "crying out" to God. It begins from the heart, doesn't have to be loud in volume; but when you've had enough of a trouble that you are going through you call to God and say "Help!"

It's often at this point that we then await God's response. We look to see what evidence there is that what we have said has been registered in heaven. God clearly says that He has heard your cry. In the same way that I thought nothing was happening when I was calling for my son, where in fact he had heard and was making his way to me, so God is working towards you. He is always working on behalf of those who love Him. You are not being ignored by God. Yesterday we saw that God has granted us a position where we can access Him at any time. The Bible also says this *"And this is the confidence that we have toward Him, that if we ask anything according to His will He hears us"* (1 John 5:14).

Father God, I thank You that You have shown Your love for me, by sending Jesus so that I can come close to You. Thank you that Your eyes are toward me and Your ears are listening out in case I am in distress. Thank You that you always hear my call and are always working on my behalf.

#Day29

GOD OF JUSTICE

"The face of the Lord is against those who do evil,
to cut off the memory of them from the earth." (Psalm 34:16)

In the 1990s I used to work for a bank near the London Stock Exchange. It was a bit of an alarming time to work in London as there were numerous bomb alerts with innocent people being killed. One such time I remember walking home to hear what sounded like thunder in the distance; but it wasn't quite like thunder. It turned out that the Baltic Exchange had been bombed with three people killed and 91 being injured.

A year later Bishopsgate was bombed with one losing their life and others injured. The branch that I worked in was unusable following that incident and never reopened for business. These were places that I walked past regularly and I wonder how different things would be if I'd been caught up in the blast. The first thing that comes to mind is of a grieving family and the woman I would never get to meet or marry. Then there are two lovely boys who would never have come into this world; things that I value more than anything in the world.

Is this sounding a wee bit dark today? We read about *"...those who do evil."* Who then is it talking about? Well, it doesn't simply refer to those who do wrong, since that is all of us; but rather people who plot and carry out evil as a part of their way of life. Yesterday we noticed how God hears the righteous; He is working on yours and my behalf. Just as God favours and protects those who honour Him; conversely those who dishonour God with evil don't come under that same protection or favour.

Yet there's more to it than that, God actually sets His face against those who plot evil, whoever they are, whatever their views or aims are.

Often people think that the use of evil will forward their cause, yet the very evil they do, draws the attention of God who will become a block to their ways. If they don't respond to His mercy and turn from their evil, they will feel the power of His wrath. Remember that kitten that was actually a lion? A lion deserves much more respect, and certainly is not safe. Jesus is called "The lion of Judah," a title that He has earned and that describes His power and His Kingship. He is the best King ever, who will fight for the cause of those who are abused and bullied and He will deal with those that make crime their means of living. His face is against them, He doesn't turn a blind eye to them or their deeds. He is a fair judge. It describes His actions on behalf of the righteous.

You know sometimes when we see evil appear to prosper we can tend to think that God doesn't deal with evil people and ask "Does He really wipe them out so much that they are no longer mentioned in history books?" Once done, a person's deeds cannot be undone and that impacts history. So what does the verse mean? People want to be remembered after they are gone for the impact they had on others, otherwise what purpose is there of having lived? Others just want to be famous. The words we read about the evil being cut off refer to His coming judgement where the memory of them will be eradicated. In the meantime the generations to follow will not be under their evil influence. To those who are scarred by the works of evil, Jesus will repair the damage made, He can heal those painful memories and bring the hurting back to enjoying life again.

Maybe you are wondering, "Can I do anything to cut off the memory of those who have done evil to me?" Yes there is something you can do. Did you know that forgiving does not mean forgetting what someone did to you? Yet in the process of forgiving someone, Jesus can make a start on healing your memory of what they did. What is forgiveness then? To forgive someone means that you no longer have hard feelings toward them. That you no longer wish they were knocked down by a bus or mauled by a hungry panther. If you like I can take you through the process of forgiveness? Over the page is a prayer space designed to take you through what forgiveness is and how you can allow Jesus to heal you from the pain and hurt of what others have done to you.

PRAYER SPACE – FORGIVING OTHERS

To forgive is to release the hard feelings you feel toward a person, so that if you were to think of them, you would not have hate, bitterness or rage towards them.

You might say:
> "But it wasn't fair what they did" or "it was not right"
> "How can I forgive? They do not deserve it."

• Forgiving someone doesn't mean what they did to you was right.
• Forgiving does not mean that they "get off free." If it is a crime they have committed they still have to answer to the law and to God.
• Forgiveness does not mean you give up all your rights, or that you have to allow that person back into your life.
• Forgiving someone does not mean you have to forget what they did.

If you decide not to forgive someone:
• It doesn't hurt the person who harmed you like you might think!
• It actually hurts only you
• It places you in emotional chains and will torment you
• It may cause you to grow bitter, angry & change you in a negative way
• It blocks the fullness of God in your life

Forgiving those who hurt you:
• Means you can step aside to let God deal with that person
• Will remove a heavy emotional burden from you
• Sets you free
• It closes a door which allows the enemy to have access to you

Forgiving allows you to say:
> "I choose to forgive even though they may not deserve it"
> "I choose to let this person go into God's hands"
> "I am not going to be their judge"

PRAYER SPACE – FORGIVING OTHERS

Take a look at these Bible verses before we pray:

Matthew 6:14-15

"For if you forgive others the wrongs they have done to you, your Father in heaven will also forgive you. But if you do not forgive others, then your Father will not forgive the wrongs you have done."

Read Matthew 18:21-35

Then Peter came to Jesus and asked, "Lord, how many times shall I forgive my brother or sister who sins against me? Up to seven times?" Jesus answered, "I tell you, not seven times, but seventy times seven. "Therefore, the kingdom of heaven is like a king who wanted to settle accounts with his servants... (See Matthew 18:21-35 for the full story)

..."This is how my heavenly Father will treat each of you unless you forgive your brother or sister from your heart."

Luke 6:37

"Do not judge others, and God will not judge you; do not condemn others, and God will not condemn you; forgive others and God will forgive you.

Forgiving others is a choice we make and not an emotional feeling
Forgiving will set you free

Father God. I now understand how important forgiving those who have hurt me is, and how not forgiving others actually hurts me even more. I want to forgive, so please come close as I need your help to say these words:

Lord Jesus, I choose to forgive _____ (say their name) for _____ (tell Jesus what they did to you). I release to you all the hard feelings that I have toward this person. Please remove every chain that is holding me back from receiving the freedom that you want me to enjoy. Please transform me by your power to live out this forgiveness today, tomorrow and every day. In your powerful name Jesus!

#Day30

A BALANCING ACT

*"When the righteous cry for help, the Lord hears
and delivers them out of all their troubles."*   (Psalm 34:17)

Step back with me into the shoes of David as he fled from one king, only to be faced with fearful circumstances before another king. Leaving home in haste, it wasn't safe even to say goodbye. His hurried departure left him with only the things he could carry; and what of his day to day existence?

If it was me I'd be in survival mode, mindful that the clock is ticking ever closer to nightfall. The pressure is on to find water, start a fire, to locate some shelter and food to keep your strength up. Which do you try to find first? If you flee to a forest and begin to build a shelter will you faint from exhaustion before you manage to finish and find food? Maybe you will find a cave, so starting a fire will be useful to keep warm, but is it near a water source? It's at this point you might realise that you need extra help.

It reminds me of an act I once saw on TV. A man had about fifteen dinner plates with a number of long sticks that were freestanding, attached to the floor. The act would begin very simply where he would place a plate on a stick and give the plate a spin. Impressive, or so I thought, until he did the same with another, spinning two at the same time! He went on and on until several plates were all spinning at the same time.

This all looked super-impressive, yet it didn't take long for the first plate that he had spun to slow down and begin to wobble. At this point the man stopped adding plates, returned to the wobbly one skilfully spinning it keeping it moving. He continued to add plates and re-spin others until all fifteen were spinning together, but now he had a full-time job. Which plate was going to go crashing to the floor first?

When life gets really busy it can feel like you no longer have control over things. Instead, like the plate spinning your time is filled keeping up with school, homework, coursework, revision, clubs, jobs to do at home, etc., causing you to feel stressed and overwhelmed.

We read that the Lord delivers His saints from *"all their troubles."* Did you know that you can hand all of your responsibilities over to God? He can be responsible for how they turn out, so that you don't have to stress about the outcome? How many troubles are we talking about? A few? Some? It actually says "all." Don't hold back, give them all to God! How do we do practically hand all of our responsibilities over to God?

We imagined what it must have been for David, called to be king, but actually in the complete opposite position. What advice would you have given David, knowing that he would one day become King of Israel? "Don't stress! You'll be king someday!" you might say. But how could that ever happen? There was little chance that David could make it happen. God would have to order David's steps and influence the situations around him. This was far beyond David's ability to control.

From David's point of view he was vulnerable and alone. But something happened… We read in 1 Samuel 22:1-2 *"David left Gath and escaped to the cave of Adullam. When his brothers and his father's household heard about it, they went down to him there. All those who were in distress or in debt or discontented gathered around him, and he became their leader. About 400 men were with him."* God was beginning to deliver him from all his troubles! We know that's what God did, he eventually became king.

But I have a million things to do! Why not simply get on with those things that are immediate or most important and ask God to fill in the gaps for all the things that you can't do? He is in charge of the outcome, so try and let go of the responsibility of how everything is going to turn out. Ask Him regularly for the things you need and thank Him when you notice He has answered; like when you're just out the door and are reminded about not forgetting something. It's Him helping you! He will provide for you. The more you depend on Him the more you will see Him helping you!

WHERE DO BROKEN HEARTS GO?

"The Lord is near to the broken hearted"   (Psalm 34:18)

When I was young we moved as a family to the countryside, to a wee island off the east coast of England. I expect I was about six or seven years old. At my new school as I glanced across the classroom, a girl caught my eye. Her name was Leanne and to me it was love at first sight. She was so pretty and kind. I wondered "Would she ever notice me?"

Fast forward a few years and there was only ever one girl I had eyes for. It seemed every day I was captivated by her beauty and she also seemed to like me too. I remember the day she kissed me in the quiet playground! It was like I was in a dream land! Unfortunately this dream was not to last for me. My family had to move back to London and as you can imagine, this came as a bit of a shock. I was very settled, happy and in love.

Heartbreak comes in many forms. Maybe it's when you pluck up the courage to ask someone out on a date, to which they reply "I like you as a friend, but..." It can also be quite brutal at times when you are in a relationship and that person breaks it off with you, or you discover they are dating someone else. Broken hearts will happen when someone moves away, a loved one dies or if you discover a person was not who you thought they were. It's a powerful emotion, love, which makes heartbreak not only distressing, but painful too. I've had to cope with a few heartbreaks and each time I felt all I could do was to lay on my bed and breathe, it was so crushing a feeling. So if you are feeling this way, God's heart is nearer to you than you think. He wants to be your comfort, to help you through this difficult time and importantly to work on mending your heart.

What is the best way to process heart-break? How do I deal with where I'm at, let alone move on with my life? There's a danger when your heart is affected in such a way, that you are vulnerable to replacing that void with something else, something negative, like eating too much, obsessing about your looks, becoming bitter or blaming those around you, a whole host of things. So you need someone to help you through, chatting about it with a trusted friend can help, although you'll need to be careful how you talk about others. Better still you can say whatever you like when you are on your own with God!

Why not take full advantage of what Jesus offers you? We read *"He is near to the broken-hearted,"* which means that He will come particularly close to help comfort you if you will let Him in. It may be that you need to release some emotions, shed a few tears and ask God to show you who He is for you at this time. Often He will speak a thought into your mind that will encourage you for the day ahead. It's very easy to allow negative or obsessive thoughts to enter, where your mind goes round and round about what they said and what you said. It's worth getting off that merry-go-round, since it's not very merry! Just see what God has for you today, and take each day as it comes.

Of course in the middle of heartbreak we really don't want to think about the possibility of meeting someone new, as the preciousness of the person we loved is at the forefront of our minds. Phrases like "There are plenty more fish in the sea," just don't help when the person you treasured is no longer in your life." Yet there will come a time when your heart is healed and you are ready to love again. So allow God to lead you close to Him, to encourage you and to make that pain fade, for He is close.

You know it's actually okay to pray and to say nothing at all! What am I talking about? Sometimes the words just won't come or the ability to say them is too difficult. If this is you, then I suggest finding a quiet place, if it's your bedroom, sit or lay just in the silence and ask Jesus to be near to you, to be close, as you have a broken heart. You don't have to say anything, just be aware that He is there with you. That's all you have to do, be with Jesus. That is praying too.

GAME OVER

#Day32

CRUSHED DREAMS

"The Lord is near to the broken-hearted
and saves the crushed in spirit."   (Psalm 34:18)

If you've ever seen the X Factor or talent shows like "The Voice," you'll have watched the features where they interview the applicants and tell you a little bit of their story. Often those who hope to progress to the latter stages have worked hard on their act and spent time performing on local stages or in clubs and bars.

At some point in the interview the presenter will ask this question, "What would it mean to you to get through to the final and win the X Factor?" More often than not, people will give the same answer, "Oh it would mean the world to me!" The feeling of doing what you enjoy, what you are good at, on the big stage means a complete transformation in lifestyle. Who wouldn't like the idea of that? Yet as people get knocked out during the closing stages of a competition like this, it is often an emotional farewell. Even though they've tried to manage their expectations and not get their hopes up, inevitably the disappointment of not achieving what they hoped for so much can leave a person feeling crushed and broken.

I remember in junior school being asked by my teacher what I wanted to be when I was older. I replied that I wanted to be a Milkman, to which the whole class laughed. My reasoning at that age was that I could do my milk deliveries early in the morning and then have the rest of the day to put my feet up! Years later I obviously developed my ambitions, as my hopes and dreams for the future became clearer.

Do you have any deep desires for your future? What do you dream of doing? Like my Milkman idea it's not something you have to decide on for a while; but maybe there's a seed of an idea in your heart that is growing concerning the things you might do in the years to come?

It's possible that we will all experience disappointments in life that leave us feeling despondent. I've had a fair few in my time and I can tell you it can really knock you back. So it's very encouraging to read these words, "The Lord is near to the broken-hearted *and saves the crushed in spirit.*" Maybe the grades that you were hoping for didn't materialise, making you wonder what options this leaves you with now. Things like re-sits of exams can feel quite demoralising or even humiliating. Let me just tell you now that your grades do not define who you are. It is your character, personality and identity in God that determines your future prospects. He will lead you to places that a person cannot reach by themselves.

When David was a boy, he was the least in his family. God sent a prophet to tell him that he would one day be King. Years later, still yet to be king he finds himself down and out in a cave, pursued for his life. Men who are similarly demoralised gather round him and he begins to lead them. David turns this band of "losers" into mighty warriors. It's a known fact that God opens doors of opportunity that we could never open on our own. So if you are feeling crushed, know that God has a plan to save your future. He has a place for you in this world, so trust Him to lead your steps.

Don't lose your dreams. He says "I love dreams and I love the dreamers, where do you think they all got it from?" God often puts dreams in our hearts. They can appear a bit foggy at first, so it takes a while for us to figure them out. He tells us, "Don't be afraid of giving them back over to Me again and again. For the dreams that I dream for My people are greater than anything this world has ever imagined."

Father God I hand to You my hopes and dreams for the future. I know that You give dreams for the future. Help me to see what Your desires are for my life. Please take me step by step through those tricky times when things don't go the way I plan. I know You will plan a way through.

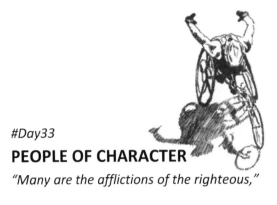

PEOPLE OF CHARACTER

"Many are the afflictions of the righteous,"   (Psalm 34:19)

Have you ever noticed that people with disabilities are the most amazing people? It's difficult to not be inspired watching those who compete in the Paralympics or the Invictus games. On hearing their stories of how they overcame adversity, we can really see what is possible if we will take things step by step, aim high and not give up. What comes across is a determination and character that demonstrates that these people have experienced life and really appreciate what is valuable in this world.

From previous devotions we've seen that everyone is vulnerable to being broken-hearted and crushed and that as God's people we are not immune from bad things happening to us in our lives. We live with frail human bodies that are finely balanced and will sometimes fail us. We also live in a world where bad things happen because of the presence of evil and the ability for mankind to exercise free will. People, motivated by selfishness and greed will always take advantage of others and we can be caught in the crossfire.

I'm sure you've experienced first-hand what harm bullies can do to those around them, afflicting others with threats, intimidation and fear. Sometimes the good are targeted because they are good and other times we're just in the wrong place at the wrong time. I remember having to vary my route home from school to avoid a lad that would intend me harm.

What do you do when things go wrong? Is it to freak out? Try and solve the problem all by yourself? Do you find someone to blame? Maybe even blame God? Or do you run to God in times of trouble? I've found that during some of the toughest times in my life that God has been the closest. He wants us to come close to Him when things get difficult.

It's important to realise that God understands. Jesus was rejected, insulted and threatened. A couple of times before His crucifixion people attempted to kill Him; once they were going to stone Him and another time they tried to throw Him off a cliff. After His death and resurrection, His disciples were constantly in danger. Many were rounded up and killed simply because they refused to renounce Jesus; but His disciples just couldn't deny Jesus! During their three years with Jesus they witnessed the evidence that He was God's Son. Not only had they heard His words and watched how he cared for those most in need, they had been with Him and seen His miracles with their very eyes. Indeed they had even touched Him with their hands after He was raised from the dead.

So because you and I are God's people, it doesn't mean that everything will be easy. Hardships will come as part of life; but God hasn't left you when these things come along. There is a verse in the Bible that says the difficulties that come our way can actually make us into stronger people, *"Consider it pure joy, my brothers and sisters whenever you face trials of many kinds, because the testing of your faith produces perseverance"* (James 1:3). I expect the last thing I would want to be is overjoyed when something bad comes my way. Yet the journey of faith that takes us through struggles often strengthens our determination and develops good character in us. These are valuable things that cannot be learnt, taught or bought. We have to go through the tough times in order to be changed. Of course many Paralympians will testify to the fact that their adverse circumstances have made them into stronger people; stronger mentally, emotionally and even physically as they have battled with their afflictions in the pursuit of competing in the games.

God does not bring evil into our lives, but in His plan to save us out of our struggles He will use what we are going through to produce something of incredible worth. So have eyes to see what God is doing in your life, cling to Him and you will see Him work some wonderful things in your life.

RACING TO OUR RESCUE

"Many are the afflictions of the righteous,
But the Lord delivers him out of them all."   (Psalm 34:19)

When I was younger, cartoons used to be on the TV a lot. One that I used to watch was Popeye, a sailor man who got super strength whenever he ate a can of spinach. The love of his life was a girl called Olive Oyl, whom he would do anything for. This was just as well, as Olive Oyl would often find herself in bother. Popeye had an arch enemy called Bluto who would seize the slightest opportunity to kidnap Olive and then place her in some precarious situation such as dangling her over a pit of hungry crocodiles.

Popeye would hear Olive Oyl's cries for help, notice her predicament and pull out a can of spinach. He would then down the contents of the can in one go to become as strong as iron. Then racing to Olive's rescue, Popeye would be presented with a set of impossible obstacles which he would deal with all at once, before making Olive safe and defeating that bully Bluto.

At the time I watched unquestioningly as this set of circumstances unfolded before my eyes; but now I think of it, in pretty much every episode Olive Oyl would end up in danger. That's a lot of troubles to face in your life. So it was a good job she had Popeye to look out for her. On the other hand, could it be that because she was Popeye's girlfriend that she always ended up at risk?

Being a Christian means that we are brought into God's family, that the wrongs that we have done have been paid for by Jesus and no longer separate us from God. We are free people!! Yet there is a spiritual enemy, the devil who is jealous of us. He hates God's people and will use varied means to attack our minds, our hearts and bodies; and much like Olive Oyl we are in need of rescuing. Does that make you want to run from the battle? It's better to be under the protection of God than not to be. We're a much easier target if we don't belong to the Living God!

The enemy would have us believe that when something bad comes our way that God is angry or has left us. Actually the reverse is true. God is often closer to us when troubles come our way. Additionally, because we are God's people the enemy wants to target us. Often the devil will try and persuade us that God is powerless to help or not interested, when in fact God is working out a solution that will make us stronger in future. Sometimes there is a process that has to be seen through as God works in us. This takes time to accomplish. It's a journey of faith that will prepare you, giving you the tools to deal with your current struggles as well as enabling you to fend off the more difficult things in the future.

We read *"Many are the afflictions of the righteous, but the Lord delivers him from them all."* We have the promise from God of being removed from not just one or two afflictions, but all of them. Much like Popeye who would never give up, no matter how many times Bluto caught up with Olive Oyl, Popeye would always set her free. I suppose he would have done well to have given Olive some training and sent her on a danger awareness course or something! Probably wouldn't have made for such an interesting episode...

You might be wondering "Is there anything that I can do to resist the attacks that come my way?" Yes indeed there is! Over the page is a prayer space that highlights the areas where we are vulnerable to attack and what we can do to prevent those attacks being successful.

Let's pray first. *Father God I thank You that You sent Jesus so that I would be free. I want to live free. Holy Spirit, please come to me now and teach me how to handle the truth of Your Word so that I am not taken down easily by the enemy. In Jesus' name!*

PRAYER SPACE - THE FULL ARMOUR OF GOD

You'll need to read Ephesians 6:10-18!

The belt of truth

This is to read and understand God's words, so that each day you will be prepared in your heart with God's perspective if fear comes knocking.

What recurring fears are bothering you?

Ask God to show you what is not true about these fears.

Ask God to give you a truth about what He is like.

The breastplate of righteousness

Having thought about God's words, ask Him how to put this truth into action (truth followed brings protection). Live it out and make it part of your life. This will protect your heart.

What truth are you going to remember when you are attacked by negative fears?

Feet fitted in readiness/Gospel of peace

Take God with you wherever you go and release God's favour on others so that others will understand and discover Jesus too.

Is there someone you know who is going through something similar?

What can you do to help them through it?

The shield of faith

Keep a barrier between you and those negative words. Reject the lies that come to mind by replacing them with God's truth about who you really are. Believe these words are true and trust Him for all you need. This will protect you from random attacks.

What do you need God to provide for you today?

Instead of worrying, let it go in your mind and depend on Him to help you with the things you can't do.

Helmet of Salvation

Having believed and received Jesus as friend and King of your life, live out your relationship with Jesus by connecting regularly with Him in conversation. This will protect your mind.

Invite Jesus into your day, or whatever you are currently doing. Welcome His presence with you as you go through your day. Renew your mind with His words everyday

The sword of the Spirit

Speak out the words of the Lord as He inspires you. Take those times to praise Him from the evidence you have discovered in His word. This will enable you to destroy the works that the devil is trying to establish in you.

What truth have you read from the Bible today? Speak it out over your difficulties and trust that God will deliver you from them all.

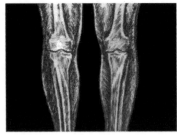

#Day35

LOOKING AHEAD

"He keeps all his bones; not one of them is broken"   (Psalm 34:20)

Have you ever had an event coming up that you're so looking forward to that you just can't stop talking about it? Maybe you've managed to get tickets to see your favourite band in concert, and although you've had to book it way in advance, the very fact that it is happening gets you excited every time you think about it. So leading up to the time of the concert, you'll be checking out their latest online feeds, listening to their songs and telling your friends random info about members of the band; because it's so exciting, your mind just can't ignore what is about to happen.

Well there's an event in history which the whole of the Old Testament is longing for. You can just sense the excitement about this event to come because references to it randomly pop up announcing what's about to happen. There are literally hundreds of them. Here's a well-known one:

> *"Therefore the Lord Himself will give you a sign. Behold, the virgin shall conceive and bear a son, and shall call His name Immanuel (which means 'God with us')."* Isaiah 7:14.

It's a seemingly random phrase that will have made sense at the time because of the way those words were used and the circumstances into which they were spoken. Yet this key phrase was actually intended to be much more than that, to speak about future events to come. Such messages are hidden for us to find, telling us what was to happen regarding Jesus' birth and what would take place in His life.

Today you have just come across one of these messages! *"He keeps all his bones; not one of them is broken."* So how is this telling us about Jesus?

Well, John the Baptist announced who Jesus was by saying these words *"Look, the lamb of God who takes the sin of the world"* (John 1:29). Jesus is known as the Lamb of God.

A lamb was significant to the people at the time because of their history when they escaped slavery from Egypt. The night before they fled Egypt Moses told God's people to kill a lamb, prepare it for eating and use its blood to make a mark over their doorposts. The blood was a sign to God to provide a covering of protection during a particular night of peril (See Exodus 12:1-51). In preparing the lamb they were told not to break any of its bones. This took place many years before Jesus was executed by the Romans, crucified as God's lamb sacrificed for us, He also would not have any of His bones broken. *"For these things took place that the Scripture must be fulfilled: "Not one of His bones will be broken"* (John 19:31-36).

Jesus has accomplished something that you and I get to benefit from. That which we read in the Old Testament, now has added meaning in the light of what Jesus has done for us. The words "He keeps all his bones," literally means "He watches over his bones," telling us that God watched over every detail of the life of His Son Jesus.

Okay so that's what it means in relation to Jesus, what then about the other, more immediate meaning? God watches over the details of your life as He would care for His own Son. Does this mean we'll never break a leg? I think you'll get that God preserved Jesus' limbs so that you and I could know Jesus was the Lamb of God, sent by Him so that we would have eternal life. Life is full of rough and tumble, where we test the limits on equipment such as trampolines and sometimes there will be accidents. So I wouldn't go out and test God and the laws of physics on that one!

However God is interested in the detail of your life. He knows what you need. How into detail is He? Why not check out Matthew 10:30, an easier job if you have a hairstyle like mine! (Go on read it!!).

Father God. Thank You that You know the detail of my day even before it happens. I entrust my day to You. Help me to go where You want me to.

#Day36

DAYS OF JUDGEMENT

"Affliction will slay the wicked," (Psalm 34:21)

I wonder what it would have been like to have been David? You know, having killed mighty Goliath the Philistine and turned the fortunes of his country to win an unwinnable battle with just one stone. Imagine walking down the street the next day after having taken down a nine foot warrior that no one else had the courage to face. I expect that is what fame is like! He would carry the reputation of a giant slayer for the rest of his life. Great if you are with your friends, not so great if you are amongst a bunch of Philistines.

Yet fame was not David's motivation for stepping out to fight Goliath. The men of Israel were so afraid of Goliath that they ran away in fear when he spoke. David wanted to demonstrate that the name of the Lord Almighty could be relied upon against evil in the most unequal of circumstances (1 Samuel 17).

In today's world we are not without those who attempt to rule over others by the use of violence, forcing others to be subject to them. Unfortunately film makers have glamorised the dark world of gangsters celebrating their crimes, thus giving them a degree of fame that they don't deserve.

Some people just seem to embrace evil. Maybe it's because of the environment they grew up in, the influences that have shaped them, or that they are motivated by money or power; but some people don't take a second thought before doing evil. They lie, steal, cheat, can be unpredictable, intimidating, often try to control others and we can feel powerless to resist them. Thankfully we too can be unpredictable! Since we have the power of the Living God within us!

We read the words *"Affliction will slay the wicked,"* communicating God's utter determination that those who do evil will not prosper forever. On the one hand God preserves those who are His own, covering them with His protection and watching over the details of their lives; whereas there is no such covering of protection from God for those who engage in evil plans. Those who do evil and make a big show of strength are actually more vulnerable than they think. Not only are they targets of God's anger, they are also undefended against other evils around them.

There's this phrase that people use: "Honour amongst thieves," which gangsters rely upon, where crooks look out for each other. It's really not true. If anyone is more vulnerable to be stabbed in the back, it is those who associate with other gangsters! The bit we read clearly states that evil will catch up with the wicked and it will be fatal. God is a God of justice who hates evil and those who use their influence to dominate and crush other people's lives.

As we said yesterday, the Old Testament is also now read in the light of what Jesus has done for us. God offers a way out for those who are willing to turn from their evil deeds. This is called "grace," which means "undeserved favour," where because of Jesus' death and resurrection a person is offered a pardon for their wrongs. God wants to transform our lives and take us out of the sin that is so harmful to us and others. However for those who reject God's offer, His judgments will be fair and evil will catch up with the wicked.

Sometimes evil will only be defeated when someone takes a stand against it in the name of the Lord Almighty. Maybe you might be feeling small like the boy David in the face of the giant, yet you have a promise of protection when you use God's way of coming against it.

Father God. I know that You hate to see evil prosper. Would You make me bold when it is time to stand against it! In Jesus' name!

GOD LOOKS OUT FOR HIS OWN

"Affliction will slay the wicked,
and those who hate the righteous will be condemned." (Psalm 34:21)

I've never had a contract put out on my life (thankfully), but for those who find their lives threatened, it must be quite a scary situation knowing someone is being paid to kill you. Why exactly was David on the run? He was fleeing an attempt on his life. It says King Saul spoke to his son and all of his servants telling them that they should kill David (1 Samuel 19:1). That's a lot of people to avoid. Thankfully David was alerted in time and he ran. From the words he wrote in verse 4 *"I sought the Lord and He answered me,"* we know David cried out to God "What are you going to do about my plight??"

Notice David didn't pick up his sword and try and take them all on, like in a scene from a Kung Fu film. He knew that God was with him, yet he had the wisdom to understand that even though his fight with Goliath was an instant victory, at other times God has a different way of doing things. To kill the first King of Israel and step up to take his place would set a bad precedent that might cause others in the future to resort to assassination when David was king. God had another way.

Do you ever ask God a question and feel you never get an answer back from Him? You know, you're praying about a decision you have to make or for an answer to something you don't understand and nothing seems to happen? Sometimes it can be that we're only looking for one specific outcome; then when the answer comes we've missed it, because our expectations were for an instant solution. The way God works will provide a better outcome than we could ever imagine.

I've known God to answer me by making an opportunity available. At other times it has felt like He's given me a choice. Either way, He is directing our paths in answer to our prayers. Often a thought has come into my head or even a dream and I've written it down. Sometimes it's the words and wisdom of other people through which God has spoken. If we are waiting for a visit from an angel or to hear the audible voice of God as His answer, we might have a long wait! Although God does speak in these ways, sometimes He wants us to hear Him often and regularly, in which case we need to develop a sensitivity to all the ways that He might speak and not limit Him to a couple.

I don't know if you have noticed in this Psalm, but we are actually reading God's answers to our cries. The words *"Affliction will slay the wicked, and those who hate the righteous will be condemned,"* can appear to be all about judgment, but actually it's His reassurance to us that God is going to deal with those who hate us. It's like He's a protective Father saying to our enemies "If you target those who are Mine, you are targeting Me and you will get what is coming to you!!"

So if you are having difficulties where you are being targeted, God is reminding you that He will deliver you. Justice will be served against those who are against you. Does this mean that you can go out there tomorrow and take them out? No, I know we see a lot of violence on the TV and it looks super impressive to take down the enemy like that. Just don't expect God to give you super strength to do it! His ways of justice are wise and as a result more permanent than our ways. Ours can often escalate a problem, causing retaliation and more pain. So talk to God and see what His solution is. Talk to other wise people too (and not just those who will agree with you!), it may well be that God will bring about a solution that will bring you lasting peace.

Father God. I feel powerless right now and I need Your wisdom to find a way through. I thank You that You are able to work in ways beyond my means to bring about a solution to my difficulties. I thank You that You are always working on my behalf because You love me and You are with me in all of my troubles. In Jesus name!

#Day38
BOUGHT BACK

"The Lord redeems the life of His servants;" (Psalm 34:22)

Imagine that the day you were born, your parents gave you a rare and expensive teddy, brand new, hardly touched by human hands. Obviously as a small child you wouldn't know any difference in the price, you would simply use the teddy for what it was made for, cuddles, sleeping, tea parties and generally taking around with you everywhere you go.

Now fast forward to the age of nine. You still love this teddy; in fact it is your prize possession. You still have no idea that it is worth lots of money, you just love "Barley" (or whatever you would call him or her) with all your heart and you can't settle to sleep without your ted.

Now imagine that one day you are out having a teddy bear's picnic and somehow you get separated from Barley. Your whole family searches for hours but no one can find your ted. You obviously are very upset and have many sleepless nights wondering where Barley has got to. Days turn into weeks and eventually you have to give up all hope of ever seeing Barley again. I'm sorry that this is a sad story, but it does get better!

Then one day, you are at work (now in your 20s) and you glance at a newspaper to see a poster advertising a teddy bear auction in town. On the poster is a familiar face! Yes it's Barley!! Your heart beats faster as you realise that you could once again be reunited with your beloved ted. So you go to the auction rooms and there in the display is Barley sitting there with a wee grin. "My teddy is pleased to see me!!" you think.

You ask the sales staff if you can have a look at the teddy, since in your mind you know how to prove whether this is your Barley. At the age of eight, Barley had an accident where he got burnt by a candle behind his right ear. It left a scorch mark which resembled a star. On checking the bear you discover the star shaped scorch mark and your heart skips a beat. You know the ted belongs to you, but no-one will ever believe that Barley is yours, so you will have to buy Barley back. But how much would you be willing to pay for him? You ask what the starting price is and are shocked to discover that bids will begin at £8,000! What do you do??

There's a word in the bit that we read today called "redeem." This means to "buy back" and takes the idea of regaining a possession in exchange for payment. Being redeemed describes what it is to know God, as well as what it is like to be separated from Him. Every person is born into this world just like that ted, needing to be bought back.

As humans we were created by God and should be His, but we have been separated from God, stolen away by an enemy who used our wrongdoings to gain control over our lives. As a distraught loving dad, God longs for us, searching to bring us back to Him.

Just as you can't put a price on that teddy because of his or her value to you, so you are of great value to God. He too was faced with a very high price to buy yours and my freedom, to bring us back into relationship with Him. He came to the earth in the form of His Son Jesus, to tell the world of the way back to Him. He then paid the ultimate price for our souls by allowing Himself to become a sacrifice as payment; His life for yours and mine. We were born into slavery, but God offers us a way to be free.

I know we've mentioned this before and you might say to me "But I know I am a follower of Jesus! I have a relationship with God!!" I'm so happy this is the case. He wants you to know you are loved.

But maybe you aren't yet a follower of Jesus and are beginning to understand that you are being given an invitation today by God to be brought home with Him into His family. Jesus has already paid the incredibly high price for you to be free, and wants you to know Him. You can do that now if you would like to. Turn over the page and see...

PRAYER SPACE

If you would like to take God up on His invitation to know Him, you can do this by praying this prayer to Him. If you can speak (or whisper) it, all the better!

Thank You Jesus for Your invitation.

I come just as I am.

I know I have done many things wrong.

I thank You for dying on the cross for me.

Cleanse my life.

Set me free from the past.

I open the door of my life now.

I receive Your invitation.

I receive You into my life.

Come in by Your Holy Spirit.

Fill me with Your peace, Your presence, Your power.

Help me to build my life on You

Thank You Jesus for hearing my prayer.

PRAYER SPACE

You are now a follower of Jesus and part of God's family!!! Why not draw, write, doodle or scribble down anything that you want to say to God...

STEPPING THROUGH

"The Lord redeems the life of His servants;
none of those who take refuge in Him will be condemned." (Psalm34:22)

I wonder what it would actually be like to step through into the world of Narnia. To be playing hide and seek, finding a secret place in a wardrobe, only to discover it goes back further than you think. Then before you know it, you are standing in a snowy wood and the animals can talk!

Obviously Narnia is not real, but just imagine if it was... stepping into a world where the lines of good and evil were more easily recognised. On the one hand there's an evil witch whose army consists of wolves, goblins, pig men, trolls and the like; whereas on the other hand Aslan the lion commands a battalion of centaurs, bears, horses, fauns, and nicer folk! Of course you would still have no idea which side the trees were on!

It says *"The Lord redeems the life of His servants; none of those who take refuge in Him will be condemned."* When we are redeemed by God we begin to understand the real spiritual battle that rages; once being under the control of darkness, before being brought into the kingdom of light. If you have ever read the Narnia books, you might have figured out that the stories told reflect the very real conflict between these two kingdoms.

So when you say that you believe in Jesus and trust that His death on the cross has set you free, it is like you have stepped into a new world where you receive a new identity. You are no longer condemned. You have joined the kingdom of light, God's kingdom and much like Peter, Susan, Edmund and Lucy you have a new identity. Only princes and princesses have access to God's throne room and that is what you now are. "Seriously?" you ask. Okay this one might take some explaining.

The Bible says that this is your new identity, *"But you are chosen race, a royal priesthood, a holy nation, a people for His own possession, that you may proclaim the excellencies of Him who called you out of darkness into His marvellous light. Once you were not a people, but now you are God's people; once you had not received mercy, but now you have received mercy"* 1 Peter 2:9-10. What does this all mean then? It means you have joined God's side and as royalty you have free access into God's presence.

Now I want you to understand the scope of what this means. You have been given power by God to command His blessing wherever you see fit. Peter, Susan, Edmund and Lucy were given royal gifts to battle the enemy and to bring healing. God also gives you gifts, so that your words will set others free. You are not under condemnation anymore, which means that you are no longer under the control of what the enemy wants in your life. You have the strength to resist doing wrong, as you are free from the slavery of sin. Of course we all still do wrong things, but now if you don't want to do those things, God gives you the power to say "no." You are not powerless to resist evil anymore because of who you are. You are a child of God. Suddenly the life of God is within you and what comes with your new identity is a purpose to see what role you have in His plan.

What else do you have power over? Negative fears come from the enemy, but you are no longer subject to his power or his lies. The only way that the enemy can get a grip on your life now is if you let him in. How do we let the enemy in? Maybe you have believed a lie that has been fed to you and now it's eating away at you from the inside? If you are feeling the pull of a negative habit in your life, it's time to recognise you have believed a lie, to discover it and reject it. Take that negative thought to Jesus and ask Him what the truth is. Ask Him who He is for you and read His words. It's like putting on a helmet over your mind so that you can discover what the reality is.

Father God. I see that through You I have access to a realm of answered prayer that I never realised I had access to before. I thank You that Your kingdom is powerfully advancing and that You want to provide for me and through me for the benefit of others. In Jesus' name!

115

#Day40

TABLES TURNED

"And the men of David said to him, "Here is the day of which the Lord said to you, 'Behold, I will give your enemy into your hand, and you shall do to him as it shall deem good to you."   (1 Samuel 24:4)

This is such an interesting twist in the story of David. King Saul continues in his murderous pursuit of David, who has managed to evade all attempts to be found. (David even finds time in his busy schedule to save the city of Keilah from the Philistines). Then one day as David hides out in the back of a cave he hears some noises. King Saul has stumbled across the same cave, not knowing that David is inside. The reason Saul enters the cave is because he badly needs a poo and well, when you've got to go, you've got to go! So Saul goes into the cave for some privacy from his 3,000 soldiers who accompany him and as they stand outside waiting and talking about the weather, it's all going on inside the cave.

As Saul gets out his newspaper and makes himself comfy, a conversation between David and his men takes place in hushed tones at the back of the cave. "This is your moment David," his men whisper. "Take out your sword, slay your enemy and end this manhunt. God has given you this opportunity, now take it!" Then as Saul goes about his business, David creeps up with a sharp sword; but instead of killing the king, he slices off a corner of his robe and returns to the back of the cave.

The disappointment is etched on the faces of his men as David returns to them with a piece of cloth, rather than the head of his foe. Worse than that, in hushed tones (like being told off by mum somewhere quiet like a library); David tells his men that it was a bad idea to kill the king.

How the tables have turned! This powerful man King Saul had the upper hand, with all the influence and means to find and kill David, yet he couldn't. David on the other hand fled with nothing, into the hands of his other enemies the Philistines. Yet God preserved His life and even gave him success enough to defend a city and to prosper. With the passing of time God had worked and against all odds, now it was David who has come out on top.

I hope you can see from Psalm 34 that this is what God wants for you too. That whilst you may have hardships, it doesn't mean that God has left you or that He is against you. He is always working on your behalf. So it is important that you work with Him and do things His way.

During his moment of victory, David could have just seen winning as his aim and assassinated the king. Yet choosing to honour God and His ways brought about the better outcome. Of course he must have been torn between what he wanted to do and what he knew God wanted. Which may be why he wrote *"Taste and see the Lord is good,"* where choosing to set aside our way of doing things in favour of God's way (even when we really want a different way) is the most worthwhile.

Take for example when worry knocks on the door, sometimes we are lured into it because it can feel productive or comforting, but actually it is only motivating us to process negative fears in our minds which are lies. If you can taste what it is to totally rely on God for the outcome, you will experience the goodness of His peace and a lasting freedom from stress. Because the truth of the matter is that God will deliver you from those things you fear will happen. So try Him out. Devote your time to Him, for He works on behalf of those that are His. Discover His words and you will begin to notice His ways and see how He is working on your behalf to turn the tables on your fears.

We're coming to the end of this devotional now. It might be that you will need to re-read bits in order to "get" some of the principles of faith that I have shared with you. Some bits need thinking through more than once to properly understand and begin to live by. I hope the prayer spaces have been useful in helping you to find that secret place with just you and God. Prayer is so much more than "hands together and eyes closed!"

So as we end our time together in Psalm 34, I just wanted to pray a blessing over your life.

May you know the blessing of the Lord God Almighty.
May you wake each day with something to thank God for.
May your soul prosper
and may you discover how great God's love is for you.

May you be blessed with the close presence of Jesus.
May you feel secure and free from anxiety and fear.
May you be strengthened with God's joy
and may the Lord lead you out from all of your troubles.

May you know the goodness of God daily.
May you always be able to find that secret place with Jesus.
May God provide for all of your needs
and may you depend on Him all your days.

May your trust of God never fade.
May you always know His will for your life.
May you see many days
and may the Lord protect you from all evil.

Your cries will always be heard in heaven.
May the power of God's Kingdom be released through your life.
May your broken heart be healed and made whole again
and may your dreams find fulfilment in God's purposes.

May you have perseverance in times of trouble.
May you enjoy the Lord's protection.
May the Lord bring justice for your cause
and may you walk with Jesus all the days of your life!

FINDING IDENTITY

If you enjoyed this devotional book, there's another one available!

This teen devotional is all about understanding the answer to the question "Who am I?" *Finding Identity* encourages you to see yourself from God's perspective.

Finding Identity will take you deeper into Psalm 139 and at the same time begin to inspire you about who you are and who you are called to be.

Over the page is an excerpt from the book...

ENCLOSED BY GOD

"You hem me in behind and before,"   (Psalm 139:5)

Are you the adventurous type? I'm thinking of those outdoorsy activities like rock climbing, abseiling, or jumping out of an aeroplane (with a parachute)? You know, brave pursuits that contain the element of danger? Well there is one such "fun" activity that I am never going to try. Even if you were to offer me a million pounds, you would not be able to make me do the pastime I'm thinking of. It's the activity of potholing. What, you ask, is potholing? I suppose you would call it extreme caving. Where you crawl down into a hole in the ground and you keep crawling as the space you crawl through gets smaller and smaller.

I've seen it on TV and it looks super scary, as people go one behind the other, on their stomachs squeezing through tight rocky crevices with just the torch on their helmet as their source of light. My biggest question about it all is "What if I get stuck? What if my shoulder seizes up or something? Or I get scared and freak out in a confined space? Who then is going to get me out? Would everyone have to reverse out??"

I guess the feeling of being in an enclosed space surrounded by rock makes me uneasy! The idea of being "hemmed in" in this verse can sound like a negative thing, trapped with nowhere to get out. This is not what is meant here, since we're told that being hemmed in by God enables Him to know us in a wonderful way. Is He around us like a bubble? Not really, that's too impersonal for God. It actually means something very friendly and positive; literally "You enclose me." This picture communicates "a surrounding" by God, yet see it in the friendliest of terms. Being bigger than us, He reassuringly wraps around us, making us feel secure in the knowledge that He is close.

Yet there's even more to it than that! It says *"You hem me in behind and before,"* meaning that He's got your back and He goes before you. When someone says "I've got your back," they are telling you that they will remain close looking out for you, thinking of your protection. There are times when negative things come at us that we aren't ready for. God is behind us shielding us when attacked. God also goes before us to check the way ahead. He guides our steps, preparing the way ahead helping us to avoid the pitfalls of life that may lay ahead. He loves to speak to us about what's ahead, encouraging us and preparing us to recognise the way He is working in our lives.

With God we are covered. He sticks with us as the most faithful friend; but remember who God is. He is the awesome and mighty Creator of the universe. If you know Jesus, your identity is as a friend of God! He placed the stars into space and multiplied 5 loaves and two fish to feed 5,000 people. He is the commander of the armies of heaven, and the One who is so utterly holy that no-one can look at Him in His full glory and live. Yet He will come close enough to enclose us, if we invite Him to.

Yesterday we talked about entering into conversation with God in a deeper way. One of the benefits of this is that you become the guy or girl that God wants to hang out with. As a result of our conversations with God, we have the Almighty with us. There is no greater identity than knowing that we are called a friend of God. Get to grips with that. Not only does God love you, He likes you too! He wants to be around you even more than you want Him! This is His choice, not because He has to.

Lord God Almighty. I want You to be with me in everything I do. I thank You that You want to hang around with me! Thank You that I can walk down the street, knowing You're near, behind me and before me. I know that when I have You with me I can be an enormous blessing to others. May I be more sensitive to the times when You want me to know that You are real close, that I may know what You are up to. In Jesus' name!

PRAYER SPACE - How do I pray?

PRAYING IS DEVELOPED
- It starts with a word
- It grows into a relationship

PRAYING IS A RELATIONSHIP
- Tell Him your thoughts and heart stuff
- Find out more about Him

PRAYING IS A PLACE OF GROWTH IN GOD
- The Spirit of God works in you
- Your life will change for the better

HANDY TIPS
Have a listen to a Christian worship song...
Take out your Bible and read slowly, thinking about what you read.
Write or draw any thoughts that come to mind in a prayer journal.
This is all best done in your own space alone with God.

Worship	Bible	Prayer Journal	Quiet place

Psalms
37, 103
23, 63, 51
126, 139
145, 46
105

PRAYER SPACE

WORSHIP PRAYER

This bit is to help guide your conversation with God in order to bring you close to Him. It's all about adoring Him with the words that you use.

THANKSGIVINGS – What big or small things have you noticed today?

ALL ABOUT GOD – What have you discovered about what He is like?

WHAT GOD HAS MADE ME – Thank God for what He has done in you.

OUR RESPONSE TO GOD – What do you devote back to God?

NOTES

NOTES

NOTES

NOTES

Like or follow us on

...to hear about previews, freebies and new publications from the Inspire series.

Available now at Amazon.

INSPIRE – A resource for busy youth workers - VOLUMES 1&2

This discussional resource is written for all those involved in youth ministry. With over 60 Bible interactive study sessions in each volume it moves chronologically through the Old and New Testament. Volume 1 tackles the big stories of the Old Testament like Noah's Ark, as well ones that may be less familiar to young people such as Job, Hagar and Eliezer.

Volume 2 continues where volume 1 left off, completing the Old Testament stories before moving on to the New. This resource is ideal for those with limited preparation time, yet want to take young people deeper into God's word and understand its applications in a more meaningful way.

© Julia Louise Hope Photography

Amy Walters Art & Design

Christian Graphic Design Artist

Amy created this logo for Paul Martin's
Furnace youth group in 2015.

For enquiries and commissions e-mail
amywaltersart@gmail.com

Made in the USA
Columbia, SC
10 February 2020